DINING IN-CHICAGO

By Karen Goldwach Stevens

PEANUT BUTTER PUBLISHING

Peanut Butter Towers　　　　　Seattle, Washington 98134

Also available in this series:

DINING IN — SEATTLE
DINING IN — SAN FRANCISCO
DINING IN — HOUSTON
DINING IN — MINNEAPOLIS — ST. PAUL
DINING IN — MONTEREY PENINSULA
DINING IN — LOS ANGELES
DINING IN — DALLAS

Cover Photography by Dale Windham

CONTENTS

PREFACE

I had always assumed that the culinary gulf that existed between the food I enjoyed when dining out and my own was largely due to the absence of a secret ingredient available only to restaurateurs. In the preparation of this book, however, I was permitted to witness the cooking procedures of many of Chicago's finest kitchens and at no time did I detect the addition of a single item with which I was unfamiliar. And I was further amazed to discover that many dishes which I assumed called for complicated preparations actually were quite simple to create. Chefs assured me that if there was any "secret" at all, it was that even the most experienced cooks can make mistakes and will give a recipe a second chance. Patience, imagination and common sense, they explained, were the special ingredients in all outstanding dishes.

All of the owners and chefs with whom I spoke were extremely generous with their advice and many of their remarks are included along with the recipes in this book. Keep in mind that the recipes themselves are reduced versions of dishes offered at the restaurants mentioned. (Some are specials, so if you visit and don't see them listed—ask.) Although the chefs at each establishment carefully evaluated these dishes for home proportions, recipe reductions can be tricky and individual judgment should be exercised for best results.

K.G.S.

FOREWORD

Dining In–Chicago—what a great title for a book. The only problem is that I gain weight just repeating it. Having once been a 254-pound fatty—now down to 170—it's no big secret that I love to eat; a national pastime rivaled only by sports, sex, and possibly dieting.

When I was asked to write this introduction, the publisher explained it would be "a collection of menus and recipes for complete meals from 21 of Chicago's finest restaurants—a book which allows those who enjoy fine dining to create gourmet meals in their homes."

My first concern was which restaurants would be included? And what would I do if author Karen Goldwach Stevens included restaurants that I didn't like? Well, I certainly didn't have anything to worry about. I have eaten in all but three of the twenty-one restaurants and eight of my top ten dining spots in the city are included in this book.

There was a time when dining out meant nothing more than getting something to eat. The majority of Chicago area restaurants prior to 1970 could best be described as pleasant with good food. And then the interior designers got their hands on a couple of monied restaurateurs and started turning out some real showplaces. Before the word glitz was out of your mouth, it was *the* byword for describing the new trend in Chicago restaurants.

All of a sudden, going to lunch or dinner had nothing to do with eating. The entire restaurant experience became a discussion of decor and which chic new designer had done it. And just as quickly, some real restaurateurs rebelled. They actually remembered that people went to restaurants for a dining experience, and that meant better-than-average food, and good service.

Today it's impossible to diet in Chicago. We now have some of the finest restaurants in the country, no mean feat considering what many other cities have to offer. The decor, in many instances, still is spectacular. But the emphasis definitely is on quality food and service. It's a miracle that Ms. Stevens managed to coerce these twenty-one restaurants to share some of their highly guarded recipes. Whether you let the restaurants serve you their dishes, or decide to try them at home, you have many happy eating treats in store for yourself—and your friends.

Aaron Gold

ARNIE'S

Dinner for Four

Fresh Trout in Dill Sauce

Watercress Soup

Sliced Tomato and Bermuda Onion Salad

Arnie's Pepper Steak

Strawberries Godiva

Beverages:
With Trout and Salad: Light Beck's beer
With Entrée: California Zinfandel

Arnold Morton, Owner
Michel Teuletcote, Executive Chef

Arnold Morton has been a familiar name in the Chicago restaurant business for years. As a Playboy Enterprises' vice president, Morton was the long-time director of the hotels and clubs division, but his real ambition was to open his own establishment as his father had done more than forty years ago. So when Playboy and Morton parted company in 1973, he teamed up with Chicago decorator Jim Miller and, one million dollars later, opened his namesake restaurant, Arnie's.

Located in the Newberry Plaza, in the midst of the Rush Street area, Arnie's excellent American/Continental cuisine and fabulous atmosphere continue to draw an appreciative and loyal following. The highly stylized decor is created by an eclectic fusion of art nouveau and art deco bronze statues, gaslight fixtures, stained glass, gilded mirrors, neon sculptures, and exotic plants. The four main areas of the restaurant—the bar, the garden room, the salon and the wicker room—surround a five-story glass-walled atrium that provides a panoramic vista for those who wish to see or be seen. "I wanted to create a restaurant that I would want to hang out in—fun, exciting, great food, beautiful decor," says Morton.

Executive Chef Michel Teuletcote received his training in his native France. He served as executive chef at several French and Bahamian restaurants before coming to the United States and has been at Arnie's since 1974.

1030 N. State Street

TROUT IN DILL SAUCE

2 fresh brook trout, 12 oz. each
3 sprigs fresh dill, finely chopped
1 bay leaf
1 shallot, finely chopped
3 oz. white wine
3 oz. cold water
Dill Sauce
1 slice tomato
1 slice cucumber
Leaf lettuce

1. Clean and filet the trout, making four filets.
2. Place filets in poaching pan. Sprinkle with dill, bay leaf and shallot. Pour wine and water over the fish. Cover pan with aluminum foil and heat. Bring to slow boil and remove from heat immediately upon boiling. Allow filets to cool in the marinade.
3. Place each filet on lettuce. Cover with *Dill Sauce* and garnish with tomato and cucumber. Serve cold.

DILL SAUCE

1 cup sour cream
3 T. white vinegar
2 t. sugar
5 sprigs fresh dill, finely chopped
Salt and pepper to taste

Put all ingredients in blender and mix.

WATERCRESS SOUP

2 bunches watercress, finely chopped
1 small celery heart, finely chopped
1/8 medium leek, finely chopped
1 small onion, finely chopped
2 t. butter
6 oz. clear chicken broth
1 quart water
1 small potato, peeled and finely shredded
Salt and pepper to taste
1 cup heavy cream

1. Sauté the watercress, celery heart, leek and onion in butter over low heat. Do not brown.
2. Add chicken broth and water, then the shredded potato and salt and pepper. Let simmer for 45 minutes. Remove from heat and stir until smooth.
3. Return soup to heat and add heavy cream slowly while stirring. Prior to boiling, remove from heat and serve.

SLICED TOMATO AND BERMUDA ONION SALAD

2 beefsteak tomatoes
2 medium Bermuda onions
Fresh crushed peppercorns
Sea salt
Crushed oregano
2/3 cup olive oil
1/4 cup red wine vinegar
2 T. water

1. Slice and peel onions and tomatoes into 1/4-inch slices. Place alternated slices on serving platter.
2. Sprinkle with peppercorns, salt and oregano to taste.
3. Combine olive oil, vinegar and water and mix thoroughly. Pour over vegetables and let stand for a short period before serving.

ARNIE'S PEPPER STEAK

24 oz. beef tenderloin, cleaned, trimmed and cut into 1/4 inch slivers
Salt and pepper to taste
1 medium onion, cut into 8 wedges
2 medium green peppers, cut into 8 pieces
8 oz. fresh mushrooms, sliced
6 oz. brown sauce
2 oz. soy sauce
2 oz. Worcestershire sauce
8 peppercorns, crushed
2 medium tomatoes, cut into 8 wedges

1. Season the beef with salt and pepper.
2. Blanch the onion and green peppers in boiling salted water.
3. Coat a large, hot skillet with oil. Add meat and brown it quickly, about 2 to 3 minutes. Add mushrooms, peppers and onion. Stir and add brown sauce, soy sauce, Worcestershire sauce, peppercorns and tomatoes. Stir briskly without boiling.
4. Serve immediately with white rice.

STRAWBERRIES GODIVA

24 large, ripe strawberries
1 cup confectioners sugar
Grand Marnier
Mint leaves

1. Roll strawberries in the sugar, place a toothpick in each one and arrange on service plate. Garnish with mint leaves.
2. Pour 1 1/2 oz. Grand Marnier into 4 brandy snifters and place before each guest. Encourage guests to dip the strawberries in the Grand Marnier and eat.

The "Bakery"

Dinner for Six

Pâté Maison

Clear Tomato Soup

Contre-Filet au Poivre Vert

Pan-Roasted Potatoes

Bakery Salad

Pears Hélène

Wines:
Sangre de Toro, Torres

Ridge Zinfandel

Louis Szathmary, Owner-Chef

Louis Szathmary defied prudence and common sense when he opened The Bakery as a store-front establishment in one of Chicago's seedier areas in 1963. The restaurant quickly earned a city-wide reputation as an "in" dining spot in an "out" location, and played a significant role in revitalizing the Lincoln Avenue neighborhood into one of Chicago's most interesting and desirable areas.

The Bakery's success continues today under the guidance of the Hungarian-born Szathmary. Dr. Szathmary, who holds a Ph.D. in psychology, describes The Bakery as "eclectic Continental with Hungarian and other Central European undertones." Blending utility with a touch of irreverent whimsy, the ambiance of The Bakery's several rooms creates a sense of relaxed informality. With no printed menus, the waiters recite each evening's dishes, and Szathmary frequently emerges from the kitchen to personally greet customers.

Though low-keyed and unpretentious, The Bakery has earned more than its share of prestigious accolades, including eleven Holiday Magazine Restaurant Awards. Szathmary's personal honors include being named Outstanding Culinarian by the Culinary Institute of America in 1974 and Man of the Year by the Penn State Hotel and Restaurant Society in 1976.

2218 N. Lincoln Avenue

PÂTÉ MAISON

1 cup onions, finely minced
8 T. lard (or chicken or duck fat)
8 oz. chicken or duck livers
2 cups (about 3/4 lb.) cooked chicken, beef, veal, pork
 or a combination—but no lamb
6 T. unsalted butter at room temperature
4 T. lard (or chicken or duck fat—do not use man-made shortening)
2 to 3 T. brandy or Cognac
2 t. *Pâté Spice*

1. Sauté onion in lard until very limp, but do not brown. Add livers, raise heat, and cook until the last trace of pink disappears from the thickest part of the thickest liver. Cool.
2. Grind the cooked meat 3 times, using the medium holes in a meat grinder.
3. Grind the livers and onion 3 times.
4. Beat the butter and lard together in an electric mixer; then, beating on a low speed, add the ground liver and meat. Beat until fluffy, then add brandy or Cognac and *Pâté Spice*.
5. Correct seasoning if necessary by adding salt or *Pâté Spice*. Chill and serve with crusty bread and pickles.

In this recipe, the method is really more important than the ingredients. Regardless of the choice you make in meats and lards, do not try to change the procedure. By no means should you combine the steps.

PÂTÉ SPICE

1 1/2 t. bay leaf, very finely crushed
1 1/2 t. thyme, very finely crushed
1 1/2 t. rosemary, very finely crushed
1 1/2 t. basil, very finely crushed
2 1/2 t. cinnamon
1 1/2 t. mace
3/4 t. ground cloves
1/4 t. allspice
1/2 t. ground white pepper
1 t. Spanish or Hungarian paprika
1/4 cup salt

1. Mix the first 4 ingredients together in a spice mortar or crush them in a deep bowl with the bottom of a cup.
2. Sift through a fine sieve 2 or 3 times, crushing whatever remains in the sieve until everything is thoroughly sifted.
3. Combine with the remaining ingredients and store in a tightly closed jar.

CLEAR TOMATO SOUP

2 lbs. veal bones
1 carrot, coarsely chopped
1 parsley root or parsnip, chopped
1 celery stalk, cut up
1/2 onion, unpeeled
5 to 6 black peppercorns
1 T. salt
1 bay leaf
1 clove garlic
3 T. sugar
1 t. butter
1 6-oz. can tomato paste
1 46-oz. can tomato juice
2 T. dried tarragon
2 T. dried dill weed
6 T. cornstarch

Liquid from 2 ripe tomatoes, chopped up and run through a blender
Fresh lemon juice to taste
Fresh dill weed (if available)

1. In a large soup pan, place the veal bones, carrot, parsley root or parsnip, celery, onion, peppercorns, salt, bay leaf and garlic. Add about 3 quarts water. Cover and cook slowly for at least 4 hours.
2. Strain into another pot. Skim top if necessary.
3. Dissolve the sugar in the butter, heating until it starts to caramelize. Pour 1 quart of stock over the butter/sugar mixture. Add the tomato paste and tomato juice. Bring to boil; reduce heat and simmer.
4. Meanwhile, cool 1 pint of the stock and bring another pint to a boil.
5. Sprinkle the tarragon and dried dill weed into the boiling stock. Let boil for 2 minutes. Strain into the simmering tomato soup.
6. Stir the cornstarch into the cool pint of stock and slowly pour into the simmering soup.
7. Add fresh dill weed if you have it. Correct seasoning of the soup with lemon juice, sugar and salt. Pour the liquid from the ripe tomatoes into the soup tureen and ladle the hot soup over it. Serve immediately.

The addition of fresh lemon juice before serving adds a tang, and using cornstarch instead of flour as a thickening agent makes a translucent and syrupy soup which is very different from other tomato soups.

CONTRE-FILET AU POIVRE VERT

6 well-trimmed sirloin steaks, 12 to 16 oz. and 3/4 to 1 inch thick,
   or 6 tenderloin steaks, 6 to 8 oz. each
1 T. *Chef's Salt*
2 T. corn oil
1 T. Kitchen Bouquet
3 to 4 T. corn oil mixed with lard, or butter mixed with oil or lard
Sauce

1. Sprinkle both sides of steak evenly with *Chef's Salt.* With a
   brush, coat both sides with a mixture of corn oil and
   Kitchen Bouquet.
2. Pan fry steaks in the shortening in a large, heavy aluminum
   or cast-iron skillet. For medium rare, fry 3 to 4 minutes on
   each side.
3. Keep steaks warm on serving platter and present with *Sauce.*

CHEF'S SALT

1 cup salt
1 T. Spanish paprika
1 t. ground black pepper
1/4 t. ground white pepper
1/4 t. celery salt
1/4 t. garlic salt

Mix all ingredients well.

SAUCE

1 cup canned consommé,
  or 1 beef bouillon cube dissolved in 1 cup hot water
1 T. flour
1 T. cornstarch
1/2 cup red wine
1 cup sour cream
3 to 4 T. milk or light cream
1 T. canned green peppercorns, rinsed and chopped
1 1/2 to 2 t. green peppercorns, rinsed and soaked for at least
  15 minutes in cold water, then drained and patted dry
1 t. Kitchen Bouquet

1. In a small pan, bring the consommé to a rolling boil. Make paste
   of the flour, cornstarch and wine and stir into the consommé with
   a wire whisk. Bring to a second boil. The sauce will be very
   thick. Keep stirring constantly while it cooks, 4 to 5 minutes.
   Remove from heat. (It should resemble a thick pudding.)
2. Put 2 to 3 T. of the sauce into the sour cream and gently fold it
   in to warm the sour cream. Now add sour cream to the rest of the
   sauce. If too thick, add a few tablespoons of milk or light cream.
   Simmer 10 minutes.
3. Add rinsed, chopped green peppercorns. Stir thoroughly. Let
   stand for at least 15 but preferably 30 minutes in a warm place in
   a covered saucepan placed in a larger pan filled halfway with
   hot, not boiling, water.
4. Just before serving, add the whole green peppercorns and the
   Kitchen Bouquet to the sauce. Serve immediately.

PAN ROASTED POTATOES

2 lbs. potatoes
1 t. caraway seed
2 t. salt
1/2 t. black pepper
1 t. paprika
3 T. lard
3 T. butter
2 T. parsley, finely chopped

1. Wash and peel the potatoes, then wash them again. Cut into uneven
   cubes, approximately 1 inch each.
2. Place potatoes in a large pot with enough cold water to cover, plus
   1 inch. Add the caraway seed and 1 t. of the salt. Bring to a boil
   over medium heat. As soon as water starts to boil, remove the pan
   from fire and let stand for 5 minutes.
3. Pour off the water, place the potatoes in a bowl, and let stand at
   room temperature until cooled.
4. Combine the remaining salt, black pepper and paprika.
5. Place the butter and lard in a large, heavy frying pan. Add the cold
   potatoes and sprinkle the top with salt mixture. Place pan over
   medium heat and cook slowly, turning the potatoes gently with
   a spatula once in a while. Fry until the potatoes heat through and
   start to turn a light golden color.
6. Remove to a serving dish and sprinkle with chopped parsley.

***If you precook the potatoes according to directions, the cubes will
be just barely cooked and will not have raw centers. If you should start
to fry them without cooling them first, they would become overcooked
and break apart.***

BAKERY SALAD WITH BOILED DRESSING

2 heads Bibb lettuce
3 tomatoes, quartered
Dressing

DRESSING

2 cups water
1 cup white vinegar
2 T. prepared mustard
1/8 t. freshly ground white pepper
1/8 t. freshly ground black pepper
2 t. salt
1/2 cup sugar
6 T. cornstarch mixed with 1 cup cold water
1 cup oil
4 cups ice cubes
Any 4 or 5, or all, of the following herbs (2 to 3 T. of each):
     Tarragon
     Dill
     Scallions
     Rosemary
     Parsley (curly or flat)
     Watercress
     Marjoram
     Sage
     Chervil
     Celery tops

1. Bring water to a boil with vinegar, mustard, black and white pepper, salt and sugar. When it boils, gently stir in cornstarch and water mixture. Bring back to boil, adjust heat to medium, and cook, stirring, until it thickens and becomes opaque.
2. Remove from heat and pour into a large bowl. Add half of the oil, stirring constantly. Then add half of the ice cubes, half of the oil again and then the remaining ice cubes. Keep stirring until ice cubes are melted. Refrigerate.
3. Add herbs of your choice and mix when ready to serve.

We don't add the herbs until just before serving because that way the dressing will keep for two or three weeks. With the herbs added it will only keep for three or four days at the most. If fresh herbs are unavailable, you may use dried ones, but moisten them first with a few drops of vinegar and water.

NOTE: For variety, sprinkle some finely chopped hard-boiled eggs
       and grated feta cheese over the *Dressing.*

PEARS HÉLÈNE

6 firm pears (d'Anjou or Wilhelm)
1 quart water
6 whole cloves
2-inch cinnamon stick
1 cup sugar
Juice of 1 lemon
3 t. tart jelly, such as red currant
6 small pieces spongecake or any leftover cake
Basic Vanilla Cream
Chocolate Sauce

1. Peel pears, leaving stems on. Cut a slice from the bottom of each so that the pears will stand on a flat surface. Remove the core from the bottom, leaving a hole big enough to turn a teaspoon in.
2. Combine the water, cloves, cinnamon stick, sugar and lemon juice and bring the mixture to a boil. Add the pears to the liquid and bring back to a boil, then reduce heat to low. Simmer, covered, until the pears are fork tender, about 1 hour.
3. Remove pan from heat and let pears cool in the liquid until lukewarm. Remove pears with a slotted spoon, place on tray, and chill in refrigerator.
4. When the pears have chilled, stuff each with 1/2 t. of the jelly and a piece of cake. Place each pear on an individual glass dish with 1/2 cup of *Basic Vanilla Cream*. Spoon *Chocolate Sauce* over each and serve.

Don't throw out the cooking syrup from the pears. Add the peelings, cores, and the pieces which were cut from the bottom and continue to cook over low heat until it turns into a thick, gelatin-like substance. This pear glaze can be used to glaze fresh or cooked fruit or pastry. It can be stored in a jar with a tight-fitting lid for two or three months in the refrigerator.

BASIC VANILLA CREAM

8 T. cornstarch
1 quart milk
3 egg yolks
1/2 cup sugar

1/2 t. salt
1 t. vanilla
3 oz. butter

1. Dissolve the cornstarch in 1 cup of the milk.
2. Beat the egg yolks slightly with a fork and add to the milk/cornstarch mixture.
3. Place the remaining 3 cups of milk in a medium-sized saucepan. Add the sugar, salt, vanilla and butter. Start to heat the mixture, stirring to dissolve the sugar.
4. When the mixture begins to boil, start to stir with a wire whisk and pour in the cornstarch mixture. Beat very vigorously with the whisk. The sauce should become thick very quickly and it may not be necessary to cook more than 5 minutes.
5. Remove from heat as soon as the cream is smooth and thick. Let cool.

CHOCOLATE SAUCE

1/4 cup unsalted butter
1 cup sugar
1/2 cup cocoa
1 cup milk
1 T. cornstarch
1/4 cup cold water
1/2 cup commercial chocolate syrup
1/4 cup brandy

1. In a very heavy saucepan, melt the butter with the sugar and cocoa until the mixture starts to caramelize.
2. Immediately add the milk, stirring constantly. The hard lumps will dissolve as the liquid comes to a boil.
3. Dilute the cornstarch with the water. Pour this in a slow stream into the boiling syrup, stirring constantly. Remove from the fire and allow to cool to room temperature.
4. Dilute with the chocolate syrup and brandy. Refrigerate until ready to use.

You may double or quadruple this recipe without changing the proportion of the ingredients and it may be kept up to two weeks in the refrigerator.

BASTILLE BRASSERIE PARISIENNE

Dinner for Six

Saucisse en Croûte

Onion Soup

Sautéed Veal Sweetbreads Chasseur

Salade Bastille

Fresh Strawberries with Sabayon

Wines:
With Saucisse: Sancere-Clos de la Perriere, 1975

With Sweetbreads: Moulin-à-Vent, Paul Sapin, 1976

With Dessert: Gratien Meyer, Vin Mousseux de Saumur

George Badonsky, Owner

Russell Bry, Chef

The idea for Bastille came as George Badonsky wandered the streets of Paris looking for an inexpensive yet authentic French meal. What he finally found was served in what the French call a "brasserie," one of hundreds that dot the city. "I realized that the brasserie was the French equivalent of the American sandwich or hamburger shop: good food, quick service, informal and relatively cheap. Then I realized that we had nothing like it in Chicago, in America for that matter. I decided then and there to open one."

While the opportunity presented itself, Badonsky scouted many similar establishments for ideas on food and decor. Upon his return to Chicago he commissioned designer Spiros Zakas to help him recreate the atmosphere and ambiance of a brasserie Parisienne. When it opened in December 1977, Bastille might well have been down the block from the Boulevard St. Germain: painted wainscoating, ship's lath paneling, funky French wallpaper, white butcher paper tablecloths, and huge authentic French posters completed the effect of Gallic insouciance.

The understated decor is reflected in the menu. "From the start, our concept was to prepare French food in a simple, uncomplicated manner. We offer a lot of grilled fish and meat, very few sauces, simple country pâtés, all complemented by good but inexpensive wines. In addition, Bastille features an innovative wine bar which offers a wide variety of vintages sold by the glass.

Chef Russell Bry studied cooking at Triton College. He apprenticed in a small classical French restaurant on Chicago's north side before coming to Bastille.

21 W. Superior

SAUCISSE EN CROÛTE

1 lb. boneless pork shoulder
1 large clove garlic
1 large shallot
1/2 T. salt
1/2 t. pepper
1 pinch nutmeg
Sausage casings
Puff pastry, homemade or frozen
Duxelle
Dijon mustard

1. Grind pork, garlic and shallot through the medium holes of a meat grinder. Mix salt, pepper and nutmeg in by hand.
2. Stuff mixture into sausage casings or roll in the palm of the hand to form sausages.
3. Grill sausages in a skillet or broil until 3/4 cooked, about 6 minutes. Let cool.
4. Roll out pastry dough to a thickness of about 1/8 inch. Cut into 5" x 5" squares.
5. Place a layer of *Duxelle* on pastry and cover with a sausage. Roll pastry around sausage and seal the edges.
6. Bake in a 350 degree preheated oven until golden and flaky. Serve with Dijon mustard.

DUXELLE

1/2 lb. fresh mushrooms
2 T. minced onion
Salt and pepper to taste
2 T. butter

1. Grind mushrooms and onions in a food processor or blender until very fine. Season with salt and pepper.
2. Sauté in butter about 5 minutes, until all the liquid is gone, being careful not to burn. Take off heat and let cool.

Inexperienced cooks must learn to concentrate on keeping their eyes on the food. Cooking requires close attention, no TV watching or chit chat. A lot can be learned from watching and smelling food cook.

NOTE: Use a very thick baking pan with the *Saucisse* or the bottoms will burn before the tops are done.

ONION SOUP

4 large onions, sliced thin
1 T. butter
2 quarts white veal stock
1/2 cup dry sherry
Salt and white pepper to taste
1 T. sweet basil
Croutons
Imported Swiss cheese, grated

1. Sauté the onions in butter until they are soft and tender but not brown.
2. Add veal stock, sherry, salt, pepper and basil. Simmer for about 1/2 hour or until the flavors have mingled. Adjust seasonings and remove from heat.

3. Top the soup with croutons and cheese. Just before serving, put soup under broiler for a few minutes until cheese has melted.

Keep in mind that most cheeses have a high salt content when melted, so be careful with your seasonings and adjust accordingly.

SAUTÉED VEAL SWEETBREADS CHASSEUR

This is a very popular item in French brasseries. Americans have been slowly overcoming their reluctance to try it and it's becoming one of our more popular items. Trust me, it's delicious.

3 lbs. sweetbreads
Blanching Liquid
Flour, seasoned with salt and white pepper
Butter
Sauce Chasseur

1. Soak sweetbreads in water to remove the excess blood.
2. Blanch the sweetbreads until they are firm enough to remove the membrane when they have cooled.
3. Coat the blanched and trimmed sweetbreads in flour seasoned with salt and white pepper. Sauté them in butter until they are golden brown and crisp on both sides. Remove from pan and pat dry on towels to remove grease.
4. Serve on platter with *Chasseur* underneath.

BLANCHING LIQUID

3 bay leaves
1 t. thyme
Salt and white pepper
Water to cover sweetbreads

SAUCE CHASSEUR

2 cups strong veal stock
3/4 cup fresh mushrooms, cut into quarters
1/2 cup frozen pearl onions
2 large tomatoes, peeled and seeded
3 T. butter
2 cups whipping cream
Salt and white pepper to taste
2 T. Cognac

1. Reduce the veal stock to about 1/4 cup.
2. Sauté mushrooms, onions and tomatoes in butter. Add to reduced stock. Add the whipping cream.
3. Reduce mixture slowly until it thickens and acquires a sauce consistency. Then add salt, pepper and Cognac.
4. Simmer sauce for a few minutes longer to burn off the excess alcohol.

This sauce differs from a classical chasseur sauce in that I add whipping cream to achieve a softer taste.

SALADE BASTILLE

We use a variety of salad greens and vegetables for this salad although our favorite is Belgian endive. Endive is not always easily available though, so use your own favorite greens with our dressing.

DRESSING

3 T. strong Dijon mustard
3 T. white vinegar
1 t. thyme
1/2 t. salt
1 cup salad or corn oil
Fresh ground pepper to taste

1. Place the mustard, vinegar, thyme and salt in a bowl and mix.

2. Add the oil slowly until it has been completely incorporated into the mixture. Season with black pepper.
3. Let stand for at least 3 hours before using.

NOTE: Due to the different consistencies of mustards, this recipe may need slight alterations in the amount of oil used.

FRESH STRAWBERRIES WITH SABAYON

Strawberries
Sabayon Sauce

SABAYON SAUCE

6 egg yolks
6 T. sugar
3/4 cup white wine
Liqueur

1. Place the first 3 ingredients in a metal bowl and beat until well mixed.
2. Place bowl over a water bath or double boiler and whip vigorously until the volume has tripled and forms a thick ribbon when it falls back into the bowl.
3. Add a touch of your favorite liqueur and serve hot or cold over fresh strawberries.

NOTE: The sauce can also be mixed with equal parts of whipped cream and then frozen to produce a wonderful sabayon glace.

Bengal Lancers

Dinner for Six

Kheema Samosa

Cucumber Raita

Nan

Tandoori Chicken

Sada Pulao

Matar Panir

Kheer

Beverages:
Golden Eagle beer
Médoc Sichel or Pinot Chardonnay

Mohan Chablani and Brahm Dixit, Owners
Brahm Dixit, Head Chef

"I heard about a small Indian restaurant that had a good, if modest, reputation," says Mohan Chablani, "and when I went there, I was so impressed with the authenticity of its food preparation that within the week I bought the place and went into partnership with the restaurant's chef, Brahm Dixit." Almost immediately, Chablani changed the restaurant's name to the Bengal Lancers and moved it from its cramped quarters on Belmont Avenue to its current location on North Clark Street where diners have enjoyed exotic cuisine from the Indian subcontinent since 1970.

Indian cuisine is broadly divided into northern and southern styles, but the many subtle differences that exist from state to state can be explained as much by the various religions and languages as by the many foreign influences that have been felt throughout India's long and interesting history. "The Bengal Lancers highlights northern Indian cuisine, which was heavily influenced by the Moguls from Persia," says Rama Deva, Bengal Lancers' menu and food consultant. "They combined their own cooking style with the many Indian spices they found—cardamom, cinnamon, cumin, ginger, turmeric and others—to create a highly sophisticated, romantic and exotic cuisine."

Indian fare is noted for its curry dishes and the Bengal Lancers' menu lists several, but Chablani emphasizes that Indians do not use commercial curry powder. "Curry powder is essentially an Anglo-Saxon invention which renders virtually the same taste to everything; many native Indians have never even heard of it. Instead, they make what they call masalas, or a combination of spices, which are freshly ground daily and vary according to their use. No true curry comes out of a jar; you'll get the real thing at the Bengal Lancers."

2324 N. Clark Street

KHEEMA SAMOSA

Samosas are deep fried pastry pockets filled with regional delicacies of India. Homemade pastry is, of course, preferred, but if time is a factor, you can use a prepared dough.

1/2 cup all purpose flour
2 t. melted butter
2 t. ground coriander
1/2 t. salt
1/3 cup warm water
2 t. flour mixed with 1/4 cup water
Vegetable oil for deep frying
Kheema Filling
Podina Chutney

1. Sift flour and mix with melted butter, coriander and salt. Rub butter into flour well. Add the water until you achieve a stiff but smooth dough. Knead for 5 minutes, and then cover with a damp cloth for 30 minutes.
2. When ready, knead dough for a few additional minutes. Divide into 12 equal parts and shape into 12 balls. Roll them into thin disks. Cut each disk in half. Moisten the edges of the semi-circles with the flour and water mixture and fold them into cones. Fill each cone with *Kheema*, being careful not to overstuff. Seal the top and all other openings completely.
3. Heat vegetable oil for deep frying. Fry samosas until golden and crisp.
4. Serve with *Podina Chutney.*

Bengal Lancers

KHEEMA FILLING

1 green chili, chopped (optional)
2 cloves garlic, chopped
1/2 t. fresh ginger, chopped
2 T. fresh coriander leaves, chopped
2 t. vegetable oil
1 small onion, chopped
1/2 lb. ground lamb or beef
1/4 t. turmeric
1/2 t. salt
1/8 t. ground cloves
1/8 t. cinnamon
1/4 t. ground cardamom
2 t. dry mango powder or lemon juice
2 t. *Garam Masala*
Chopped coriander leaves for garnish

1. Grind the chili, garlic, ginger and coriander leaves to a smooth paste. Add 1 T. water if necessary.
2. Heat oil in skillet. Lightly sauté onions. Add seasoned paste and cook 2 minutes.
3. Add meat, turmeric, salt, cloves, cinnamon, and cardamom. Simmer on low heat until all the liquid dries up. Break up any lumps that may have formed. Add mango powder or lemon juice and *Garam Masala.* Set aside to cool.
4. Fill the pastry cones and fry. Sprinkle with coriander leaves before serving.

Fresh coriander leaves are available in Indian specialty shops and also in Mexican shops as cilantro or in Chinese shops as Chinese parsley.

GARAM MASALA

A *Garam Masala* is a mixture of hot spices used in many Indian recipes. There are several varieties which differ in degree of spiciness and types of spices used. This one is mildly spiced.

3 oz. coriander seeds
1 oz. cumin seeds
1/4 oz. fenugreek seeds
1 oz. cloves
2 oz. cardamom seeds (preferably brown cardamom)
1/4 t. mace
1/4 t. nutmeg
1 oz. cinnamon
1 oz. black pepper

1. Roast coriander, cumin and fenugreek seeds separately for a few
   minutes until they give off a rich aroma.
2. Combine with all other ingredients and grind.
3. Pass the mixture through a sieve and store in an airtight jar.

NOTE: Roasting the ingredients separately is important since each
        gives off its characteristic aroma at a different time.

PODINA CHUTNEY

1 1/2 cups mint leaves, chopped
2 green chilis
1/2 t. ground coriander
1/2 t. ground cumin
1 1/2 T. lemon juice
1 small clove garlic, chopped
Salt to taste

1. Blend all ingredients in a blender. Add a few tablespoons of water
   to make a smooth paste.
2. Bottle and refrigerate.

***Some of the spices and herbs used in this and other recipes may
be new to you but they're readily available at Indian specialty stores
and many supermarkets.***

TANDOORI CHICKEN

1 T. ground coriander
1 T. ground cumin
1 T. garlic powder
1 T. ground ginger
1 T. salt
1 t. ground cardamom
1 t. black pepper
1/4 t. turmeric
1/2 t. red or orange food coloring
1/4 t. cinnamon
1/4 t. red pepper (optional)
1/4 t. ground nutmeg
1/4 t. mace
1/4 t. ground cloves
1/2 cup lemon juice
1/2 cup yogurt
1 T. vinegar
1 T. vegetable oil
3 lb. fryer, or 3 lbs. legs and breasts
3 T. butter
1/4 t. saffron
1 T. ground dry mango powder mixed with 1/4 t. salt
1 onion, sliced into rings
Lemon wedges

1. Combine all ingredients except chicken, butter, saffron, mango powder, onions rings and lemon wedges. Set aside.
2. Skin, wash and clean the chicken. Pierce all over with a fork. Make deep cuts in the chicken, then rub with spice mixture. Refrigerate for 24 to 48 hours. While marinating, turn chicken pieces a few times and rub in paste gently.
3. One hour before cooking, remove chicken from refrigerator and let sit at room temperature. Preheat broiler.
4. In a small saucepan, warm butter and add saffron. Set aside.
5. Place chicken in baking tray. Broil for 10 minutes. Baste with saffron butter.
6. Broil for another 10 minutes and baste again with saffron butter. Broil a few minutes more until chicken is tender. Sprinkle with mango powder and serve with onion rings and lemon wedges.

SADA PULAO

This Persian rice dish was introduced to India by the Mogul kings. Over the generations, the Indians adapted it to their cuisine, although the choice of spices and other items still varies regionally.

4 T. butter
1 onion, thinly sliced
1 onion, finely chopped
1/2 t. cumin seed
5 whole cardamom pods
1-inch stick cinnamon
5 cloves
10 black peppercorns
1 cup rice
3 cups water
Salt to taste

1. Heat 2 T. butter in a skillet. Add the sliced onion and sauté until golden. Remove onions and set aside for garnish.
2. Heat remaining 2 T. butter in skillet. Add chopped onions and sauté until golden.
3. Add cumin seed, cardamom, cinnamon, cloves and peppercorns. Cook 2 to 3 minutes. Add rice and fry 2 minutes.
4. Add water and salt and mix well. Bring to a boil, stirring occasionally while the rice cooks. Garnish with fried onions.

CUCUMBER RAITA

1 medium cucumber
2 cups yogurt, whipped
1/2 t. black pepper
1/8 t. chili powder (optional)
1 t. salt
1/8 t. ground mustard

1. Peel and shred the cucumber. Place it in a colander and allow to drain 1 hour.
2. In a bowl, combine the cucumber and all other ingredients except mustard. When combined, sprinkle with the ground mustard.
3. Place mixture in refrigerator until ready to use.

NAN

1/2 cup yogurt
1/2 cup milk
1/2 t. baking soda
1 t. sugar
4 T. butter
2 eggs, lightly beaten
3/10 oz. packaged dry yeast
3 cups white flour
1/2 t. salt
1/2 t. poppy seed

1. Warm yogurt in a saucepan and stir in milk, mixing thoroughly. Remove from heat. Add baking soda, sugar, 2 T. butter, eggs and yeast.
2. Sift together the flour and salt. Make a well in the flour and gradually add the yogurt mixture. Knead the mixture 15 to 20 minutes or until smooth and elastic. Brush the dough with some of the remaining butter and cover with a warm, damp cloth. Set aside in a warm place for 3 hours, or until the dough has risen to twice its size.
3. Dust hands with flour. Knead the dough again for a few minutes and divide into 6 balls. Roll each ball into a 10 inch pancake. Pull each pancake gently to give it an oval shape. Cover with a damp cloth for 20 minutes.
4. Heat a griddle until very hot. Mix 2 T. butter with the poppy seed. Brush one side of the Nan with the mixture and the other side with warm water. Place the warm water side on the griddle for 1/2 minute. Remove from the griddle and place Nan under the broiler for about 2 minutes.

***Nan is a flat, oval-shaped bread baked in a tandoori oven. The people of Punjab, where this recipe originates, are among the few Indians who bake leavened bread. It is an excellent accompaniment to *Tandoori Chicken.* ***

MATAR PANIR

***This is a soft Indian cheese and green pea curry. It is especially
popular with vegetarians.***

1/2 gallon milk
1 cup whipping cream
Juice of 2 lemons
1/4 cup butter
1 t. chopped fresh ginger
5 cloves garlic, chopped
1 large onion, chopped
2 large tomatoes, scalded, skins removed, and chopped
1 t. turmeric
1/4 t. red pepper (optional)
1 t. *Garam Masala* (see *Kheema Samosa* recipe)
2 cups green peas
1 t. sugar
Salt to taste
1/4 cup chopped fresh coriander leaves

1. Mix the milk and cream in a saucepan. Bring mixture to a boil
   and add lemon juice. When milk curdles, let it stand for a while.
   Drain the milk through a colander, reserving the liquid (whey)
   for making the sauce.
2. Hang the curd (cheese) in a cheesecloth bag over the sink for 6
   hours to drain away any liquid.
3. When ready, knead the cheese well until smooth and creamy.
   Spread on flat surface in a 1/4-inch thick layer. This can be done
   by rolling the cheese into a ball, then flattening it, gently, on a
   piece of aluminum foil. Cut cheese into 1-inch cubes.
4. Heat butter in a skillet. Fry the cheese cubes until light golden.
   Drain on paper towels and keep covered until needed.
5. Add ginger, garlic and onions to the butter. Cook for 10 minutes.
   Add tomatoes, turmeric, red pepper and *Garam Masala.* Cook an
   additional 5 minutes.
6. Add 4 cups reserved whey and boil for 3 minutes. Lower heat
   and simmer for 10 minutes over medium-low heat. Stir
   occasionally.
7. Add peas, sugar, salt, and half the coriander leaves. Cook, covered,

over medium-low heat until peas are tender, about 15 minutes.
Stir occasionally while cooking.
8. Uncover pan and add the fried cheese cubes. Cook over low heat
for 6 to 7 minutes. Sprinkle with remaining coriander leaves.

KHEER

***This rice pudding is served by Hindus on religious occasions and
is also prepared as an everyday sweet.***

1/4 cup long grain rice
3 cups milk
3 cups whipping cream
3/4 to 1 cup sugar
Pinch of salt
3 T. raisins
4 T. blanched almonds
Few drops rose water
Seeds from 10 cardamom pods, crushed
2 T. unsalted pistachio nuts

1. Wash rice in cold water. Drain and set aside.
2. Combine milk and cream in a saucepan. Bring to a boil. Add rice and
cook over medium heat until rice is tender.
3. Add sugar and salt. Stir and continue to cook over medium-low heat
until mixture thickens to pouring consistency, about 10 minutes. Add
raisins and almonds. Mix well. Add rose water and stir a few times.
4. Pour mixture into individual dessert bowls and sprinkle each with
crushed cardamom seeds and pistachio nuts. Serve either at room
temperature or cold.

The Berghoff

Dinner for Six

Berghoff Sour Cocktail

Flaedle Soup

Steak Salad

Ragout à la Deutsch

Creamed Spinach

Plum Cake

Wines:
Pinot Noir Goldherbst
Chassy Côtes du Rhone, 1976

The Berghoff Family, Owners
Steven Nagy, Executive Chef

Sixty-one years after Chicago was incorporated as a city, Herman J. Berghoff, Sr. opened the original Berghoff Restaurant and Cafe. Now the third generation of Berghoffs is maintaining the old world atmosphere much as it was at the turn of the century.

Efficient, no nonsense waiters, clad in vintage German service tuxedos, bustle about the large quarter-sawn oak paneled dining room. Solid oak tables, carbon filament lightbulbs, huge beveled mirrors and stained glass wall partitions add authenticity to the old world German ambiance.

Although the menu no longer consists exclusively of German cuisine, regular customers know they can count on such seasonal German specialties as Hasenpfeffer, Rehbraten and Kalter Autschnitt in addition to the usual German favorites.

Daryl Fenton, who shares the managerial duties with Lorrin Barbero, believes that Berghoff's has avoided becoming an anachronism by maintaining its quality and high standards. "The key to a successful restaurant is to meet or exceed expectations in food, service and ambiance. Berghoff's has done that for eighty years and it's our business to see that it continues that way."

Executive Chef Steven Nagy received his primary training in Budapest and Vienna and worked in Austria, Germany and Switzerland before coming to the United States. As Executive Chef at Berghoff's he supervises a staff of forty and on an average day prepares as many as 4,500 lunches and dinners.

17 W. Adams

BERGHOFF SOUR COCKTAIL

1 jigger high malt beer such as Beck's or Heineken's
1 jigger bourbon
1 dash of fresh lemon juice
1 t. sugar
Ice

Fill blender with ice and add all ingredients. Blend at high speed, then strain into cocktail glass.

FLAEDLE SOUP

Consommé, homemade or canned
Flaedle Pancakes

PANCAKES

1/3 cup flour
10 oz. milk
Pinch of salt
4 eggs
1 oz. chives, chopped
5 oz. butter

1. Mix flour, milk and salt to smooth paste. Add eggs and chives and mix for 1 minute.
2. Heat 1 oz. butter in a 10-inch frying pan. Add 4 oz. of the pancake mixture to the pan and sauté until golden brown on both sides. Remove and let cool for 30 minutes.
3. Cut *Pancakes* into julienne strips. Place strips in soup bowl and pour hot consommé over them.

STEAK SALAD

1 lb. beef tenderloin, end cut, cut into small cubes
Salt and pepper
Lettuce
Watercress
French endive
Avocado, sliced
Black olives
Dressing

1. Season meat with salt and pepper. Grill until medium or medium rare and let cool for several minutes.
2. Arrange lettuce, watercress and endive along with a thin slice of avocado on each plate.
3. Place meat on top of salad, add a black olive as garnish, and pour on *Dressing* when ready.

DRESSING

1 cup mayonnaise
1 cup tartar sauce
1 t. mustard
1 t. sugar
1 1/2 oz. Rhine wine
1 1/2 oz. spinach, cooked and chopped
2 egg yolks
Salt and pepper
Juice from wedge of lemon

Mix all ingredients thoroughly and pour over salad.

RAGOUT À LA DEUTSCH

1 3/4 lbs. sirloin, cut into 1/2 oz. strips
2 T. butter
1/4 lb. green pepper, diced
1/4 lb. onion, diced
1/4 lb. mushrooms, sliced
1/2 pint brown gravy
1/2 cup dry white wine
5 oz. jar pimentos
Salt
Dash of Tabasco sauce
Dash of Worcestershire sauce

1. Heat 1 T. butter in skillet and add beef. Sauté until brown.
2. Sauté vegetables in remaining butter and add to beef.
3. Add gravy, wine and pimentos. Season with salt, Tabasco and
   Worcestershire sauce.
4. Cook over low heat for about 30 minutes or until done.

***Berghoff's is fairly unique in that we still do all of our
own butchering. No one has better quality food. Some may be
more elegant, but we don't cut any corners. We use the
best of everything.***

***Over the years we've received many compliments, the
sheer volume of our business being one in itself. But I think the
highest compliment we ever got was from the Lord Mayor of
Heidelberg who, after dining here recently, told us that with the
exception of his mother's, our sauerbraten was the best
he'd ever eaten.***

CREAMED SPINACH

2 oz. bacon, minced
1 oz. butter
Flour
1/2 pint scalded half-and-half
1 lb. spinach, cooked and chopped

1. Sauté the bacon until crisp. Add butter and sufficient flour to make a smooth roux.
2. Add scalded half-and-half and simmer for 10 minutes.
3. Combine with spinach and mix thoroughly. Serve immediately.

PLUM CAKE

1 lb. sugar
1 lb. butter
1 oz. salt
3 lbs. bread flour
7 oz. yeast
1 1/2 lbs. cake flour
5 or 6 whole eggs
5 cups milk
Topping
Apricot Jelly

1. Place the sugar, butter, salt and flour in mixing bowl.
2. Dissolve the yeast into a mixture of the eggs and milk and add to the mixing bowl. Mix until the dough is smooth.
3. Let the dough rise until double in size. Place in a greased 18" x 26" baking dish and apply *Topping*. Let dough rise 1 hour more.
4. Bake at 350 degrees for 35 minutes.
5. When baking is completed, glaze with apricot jelly.

TOPPING

Pitted plums
10 oz. sugar
1/4 oz. cinnamon

1. Arrange plums on top of dough and sprinkle with sugar and cinnamon.

Dinner for Four to Six

Bookbinder Red Snapper Soup

Cape Cod Coleslaw

Pampano-Papilote à la Drake

Potatoes au Gratin

Slim Strawberry Delight

Wines:
Pinot Chardonnay, Almaden

Macon Blanc Villages, Louis Jadot

Piesporter Goldtropfchen, Riesling Waldow

The Drake Hotel, Owner
K. Bud Okubo, Executive Chef

The Cape Cod Room in the Drake Hotel has been as much a favorite with Chicagoans as it has been with travelers since its opening in 1933. The quality and variety of its seafood has earned the Cape Cod Room a well-deserved national reputation and numerous awards, including its twenty-fourth Holiday Magazine Restaurant Award.

The rustic New England ambiance was created by the late Massachusetts artist Peter Hunt, who once said that the restaurant was one of his most satisfying creations. Hunt accented the split level interior with lobster traps and chowder kettles, copper ornaments, buoys, captain's chairs, an old fashioned pot-bellied stove, and large hand-painted murals and maps. Off to the side sits one of the Cape Cod Room's most popular features: the nine-stool oyster bar which offers oyster and clam stews, platters of fresh shellfish and the restaurant's famous Bookbinder Red Snapper Soup.

Executive Chef K. Bud Okubo took over in 1977 from retiring Executive Chef John Kaufmann, who had been with the restaurant since its 1933 opening. Chef Okubo had served as sous-chef under Kaufmann for twenty-two years.

The Drake Hotel, Michigan Avenue and Walton Street

BOOKBINDER RED SNAPPER SOUP

1/2 cup onions, diced
1/2 cup celery, diced
1 cup green pepper, diced
2 T. butter
2 pints fish stock
1/2 cup sherry wine plus 2 oz. sherry wine
1 cup red snapper, diced
1 pint tomato sauce
1 quart brown sauce
1 t. Worcestershire sauce
1/2 t. salt

1. In a large saucepan, sauté the onions, celery and green pepper in butter until onions are clear.
2. Add fish stock and 1/2 cup of sherry. Cook on low heat for 25 minutes.
3. Add red snapper and cook for 10 more minutes.
4. Add tomato sauce, brown sauce, Worcestershire sauce and salt. Simmer for 5 minutes.
5. Lace soup with 2 oz. of sherry and serve immediately.

This has been one of our most popular items over the years. We prepare between thirty and forty gallons every day, depending on anticipated demand, and we rarely have any left over. If there is a secret to its preparation, it's in the fish stock, which must be fresh.

POMPANO-PAPILLOTE À LA DRAKE

1/2 t. shallots, chopped
1/2 cup fresh mushrooms, sliced
1/2 cup cooked lobster, diced
2 T. butter
6 7-oz. filets of pompano
6 oz. red wine
6 oz. water
1/2 t. Worcestershire sauce
1/2 t. salt
1 sheet parchment paper (available at most supermarkets)
Oil

1. Sauté shallots, mushrooms and lobster in butter for 5 minutes.
2. Place filets in pan and add wine, water, Worcestershire sauce and salt. Poach for 20 minutes.
3. From parchment paper cut 6 valentine hearts, 22 inches wide and 14 inches long. Brush each heart lightly with cooking oil. When the filets are ready, place them individually on the left-center section of each heart. Cover each filet with equal amounts of sauce from the cooking pan, then fold the right side of the paper over the filet and make a seal by folding the edges together.
4. Place individual filled hearts, sealed edges down, in a baking sheet. Bake in a preheated 350 degree oven until each bag puffs up.
5. Serve pompano in the bag.

CAPE COD COLESLAW

6 cups shredded cabbage
2 T. cider vinegar
2 T. oil
1/3 cup sour cream
1/3 cup mayonnaise
3/4 t. salt
1/4 t. pepper

1. Pour vinegar and oil over cabbage and mix well.
2. Blend in remaining ingredients.
3. Chill thoroughly before serving.

We serve a lovely house salad here too, but our coleslaw has been a particular favorite with our customers for years.

POTATOES AU GRATIN

6 medium potatoes
1/3 cup cream (or half-and-half)
1/2 cup milk
Salt and pepper to taste
1/2 cup grated Parmesan cheese
Paprika
2 T. melted butter

1. Peel the potatoes and cook in boiling water for 10 to 15 minutes. Allow to cool, then chop.
2. Combine cream and milk in saucepan and bring to boil. Add potatoes and season to taste. Cook on medium heat 10 to 15 minutes.
3. Lightly grease a shallow baking dish and spread mixture into it. Spread cheese over top and sprinkle with paprika. Add butter over top and brown under broiler.

SLIM STRAWBERRY DELIGHT

1 cup fresh strawberries, sliced
1 T. plus 2 oz. sugar
1 t. lemon juice
4 oz. Dannon plain yogurt
2 oz. baker's cheese
1 egg yolk
Pinch of salt
1/2 lemon rind, grated
4 oz. whipping cream
1 egg white
6 whole strawberries
1/2 cup toasted pecans, chopped
1/2 cup sweet chocolate, shaved

1. Place sliced strawberries in a bowl. Combine 1 T. sugar with the lemon juice and pour over strawberries. Let rest 20 minutes.
2. Mix the yogurt, cheese, egg yolk, salt and lemon rind.
3. In separate bowl, whip the cream briskly until it stands by itself.
4. In another bowl, beat egg white, gradually adding 2 oz. sugar.
5. Fold egg white and whipped cream in roughly equal parts into yogurt mixture.
6. To serve, spoon alternate layers of sliced strawberries and yogurt mixture into a champagne glass. Top with pecans and whole strawberries. Sprinkle with shaved chocolate.

Dr SHEN'S

Dinner for Four

Alaskan King Crabmeat in Lettuce Roll

Jade Soup with Tofu and Spinach

Mongolian Beef with Steamed Rice

Fresh Asparagus Sauté with Oyster Sauce

Sugar Spun Apples

Wine:
Wan Fu

Dr. Philip Shen, Owner
En Po Wang, Executive Chef

"I had two objectives in mind when I opened Dr. Shen's," says owner Philip Shen. "First, to satisfy the better educated and more health conscious diners of today by serving the finest Chinese cuisine in the Sing Fah style—that is, using no additives and no saturated fats—and second, to create an ambiance seldom known to Chinese restaurants in which to offer it." Few who have dined there would argue that Dr. Shen has failed to accomplish his goals.

Probably no other Chinese restaurant in the country can match the spectacular atmosphere created by Dr. Shen's unusual mixture of classical Chinese artifacts, modern artwork and art deco accouterments. Red lacquered rattan chairs, huge porcelain Buddhas, and ivory and jade objets d'art successfully coexist with the many contemporary touches. The restaurant's five dining rooms, each with its own distinctive motif, surround and overlook a jade garden. "We hope that it's a little like dining in a very chic museum and that we can titillate your sense of taste and sight at the same time," says owner Philip Shen.

Dr. Shen's menu spans the spectrum of regional Chinese cuisine, all of it prepared with an eye on the nutritional benefits. Shen, who has his doctorate in biochemistry and food chemistry, emphasizes that the traditional Chinese recipes do not suffer as a result. "All great cuisines change and improve over time and Chinese cooking is no exception. We use no MSG or other additives, instead substituting natural spices and flavorings to compensate. The end result is not only delicious, but much healthier. We call this new approach to Chinese cuisine 'Sing Fah.' "

Executive Chef En Po Wang was born in Taiwan and trained in the kitchens of a master chef there. He held positions in New York and Washington, D.C. before coming to Chicago as head chef at Abacus, Shen's other restaurant, and currently supervises the kitchens of both establishments.

1050 N. State Street

ALASKAN KING CRABMEAT IN LETTUCE ROLL

4 leaves romaine lettuce
Oil
1/2 oz. bean threads
3 oz. crabmeat
1/2 oz. carrots, chopped
1/2 oz. green pepper, chopped
1/2 oz. bamboo shoots, chopped
1 oz. water chestnuts, chopped
1 t. pale dry sherry
1 T. light soy sauce
Dash white ground pepper
1/4 t. salt
1/4 t. sesame oil

1. Remove ends of lettuce leaves so they look even and arrange on serving plate. Set aside.
2. Heat oil in a wok or deep skillet to 375 degrees. Drop in bean threads and cook until they fluff. Remove them from wok, break them apart and line serving plate with them.
3. Heat oil in wok back to 350 degrees. Place all chopped ingredients in wok and stir.
4. Stir in sherry, soy sauce, pepper, salt and sesame oil. Stir briskly; cook for 2 to 3 minutes.
5. Place hot portions of the crabmeat mixture on individual lettuce leaves and roll up. Serve immediately.

JADE SOUP WITH TOFU AND SPINACH

Tofu is a custard-like cake of soybean curd which is extremely high in protein and therefore often used as a meat substitute. This soup can be an excellent vegetarian dish with the elimination of the chicken stock.

2 3/4 cups water
10 oz. chicken stock
1 cake tofu, cut into 3/4-inch chunks
1/4 lb. spinach, chopped
1 t. salt
Dash white ground pepper
1/4 t. sesame oil
1 t. light soy sauce
2 T. cornstarch paste (2 parts cornstarch to 1 part water)
1 egg white, beaten

1. Combine the water and chicken stock and bring to boil.
2. Add tofu and spinach, salt, pepper, sesame oil and soy sauce. Stir and adjust seasoning.
3. Stir in cornstarch mixture until mixture thickens slightly.
4. Mix in the egg white; stir and serve immediately.

***Tofu is available at most supermarkets and Chinese specialty stores.

MONGOLIAN BEEF

Mongolian beef was introduced to China during the Mongolian invasion when tribesmen hunted animals for food en route. Except for more sophisticated cooking methods, today's Mongolian beef retains many of the characteristics of the earlier version.

1 lb. flank steak
1/2 t. baking soda
2 t. sugar
1 T. light soy sauce
1 T. cornstarch
1 T. water
2 T. oil
1/2 t. sesame oil
1/4 cup oil
3 slices ginger, shredded
1 bunch green onions, cut into 1 1/2-inch lengths
2 T. oyster sauce
1 T. rice wine or pale dry sherry
1 T. dark soy sauce
1 dash ground white pepper

1. Thinly slice flank steak with the grain into 1 1/2-inch wide pieces.
2. Combine baking soda, 1 t. sugar, light soy sauce, cornstarch, water, 2 T. oil and sesame oil. Place steak pieces in mixture and marinate for 1 hour.
3. Heat wok to almost red hot and pour in 1/4 cup oil. Add ginger and stir for about 5 seconds.
4. Add beef and stir quickly for 30 seconds, then the green onions, stirring for another 30 seconds.
5. Stir in 1 t. sugar, oyster sauce, rice wine, dark soy sauce, and pepper. Cook for 10 seconds and serve immediately.

FRESH ASPARAGUS SAUTÉ WITH OYSTER SAUCE

1 lb. fresh asparagus
2 T. oil
1 T. light soy sauce
1 t. pale dry sherry
1 t. oyster sauce
1/4 t. sugar
1/2 t. sesame oil
1 T. cornstarch paste (2 parts cornstarch to 1 part water)

1. Snap off tough ends of the asparagus stalks. Cut into 2-inch diagonal pieces.
2. Heat the wok. Add oil and heat until it is hot but not smoking. Add the asparagus and stir fry for about 1 minute.
3. Add soy sauce, sherry, oyster sauce, sugar and sesame oil and stir.
4. Thicken mixture with the cornstarch paste and serve immediately.

Try adding sliced abalone or Chinese mushrooms for variety.

SUGAR SPUN APPLES

1 egg
1/2 cup plus 2 T. cold water
1 cup all purpose flour
2 medium sized apples
12 ice cubes plus 1 quart water
3 cups plus 1 T. vegetable oil
1 cup sugar
1/4 cup cold water
1 t. sesame seeds

1. Beat egg and water together and add to flour, stirring constantly with a large spoon until you have a smooth batter.
2. Cut the apples into quarters. Peel off the skin and cut away the cores. Then cut the quarters into eighths.

3. Coat a large serving platter with oil and prepare a large bowl filled with 1 quart of water and the ice cubes.

4. Arrange the remaining ingredients within easy reach.

5. In a 2 to 3 quart saucepan, heat 3 cups of vegetable oil until a haze forms above it or it reaches 375 degrees.

6. Meanwhile, in a 12-inch wok or 10-inch skillet, heat 1 T. oil with the sugar and 1/4 cup of cold water. Bring to a boil over high heat, stirring only until the sugar dissolves. Cook mixture briskly without stirring until syrup registers 300 degrees. Then stir in sesame seeds. Turn heat down to lowest point.

7. Drop 8 of the apple wedges into the flour and egg batter. Stir them to coat thoroughly. With a slotted spoon, transfer the apples to the saucepan of heated oil and deep fry them for 1 minute or until they turn light amber.

8. Lift apples out of oil and transfer to the wok. Stir the wedges to coat them with the syrup.

9. Using a slotted spoon, lift the apples out of the syrup and drop them one at a time into bowl of ice water. The syrup will harden instantly and enclose each piece of apple in a clear, brilliant glaze.

10. Transfer the finished spun apples to the greased platter and repeat process with next 8 wedges.

Serve the apples as quickly as you can. The candy glaze will soften if they are allowed to stand for long.

NOTE: Bananas may be substituted for apples, in which case you cut the bananas into 1-inch sections.

DORO'S

Dinner for Four

Scampi al Vino Bianco

Stracciatella Florentina
(Spinach and Shredded Egg Soup)

Fettucine Alfredo

Insalata Primavera alla Doro's
(Doro's Salad)

Scallopini alla Sorrentina

Carciofini Dorati
(Breaded Artichokes)

Zabaglione alla Doro's

Wine:
Corvo or Verdecchio

Harry Menick, Frank Scoby, Herbert Schelly, Owners

Armando Massimini, Head Chef

The origins of Doro's are simple: "We didn't feel there was a restaurant in Chicago that prepared northern Italian food the way we liked it," says owner Harry Menick. "So my partners and I opened one that did."

"The differences between northern and southern Italian cuisine lie mainly in the preparation. The northern style uses less oil and tomato and a lighter touch of garlic. It also relies more heavily on the use of butter and cream. Preference is all a matter of taste," says Menick.

Like all fine restaurants, Doro's emphasizes its commitment to only the freshest and best foods. "We even make all of our own pasta here on an imported machine. Very few other restaurants have one."

Nearly all of Doro's specialties are cooked tableside, and diners are encouraged to enjoy a leisurely meal. "We don't rush people in and out; we expect them to savor the experience by staying two-and-a-half or three hours."

Head Chef Armando Massimini began his cooking apprenticeship at sixteen and by twenty-seven was already the head chef at the famed Excelsior Hotel in Rome. After coming to the United States in 1961, he worked at the Park Shenly Hotel in Pittsburg and New York's Giambelli's Restaurant. He came to Doro's in May 1974.

871 N. Rush Street

SCAMPI AL VINO BIANCO

2 T. oil
1 clove garlic, finely chopped
4 clams in shells
1 cup dry white wine
6 T. butter
12 jumbo shrimp, shelled and deveined
3/4 cup chicken stock
1/2 cup clam juice
Salt and white pepper
1 t. flour
4 T. chopped parsley

1. Add oil to pan and heat. Add garlic and clams and cook over medium heat until clams begin to open.
2. Pour off oil and deglaze pan with white wine.
3. Add butter. When melted, add shrimp and cook for 1 - 2 minutes. Add stock, clam juice, a pinch of salt and white pepper.
4. Mix in the flour and cook an additional 1 - 2 minutes or until the shrimp is pink and firm. Sprinkle mixture with parsley.
5. To serve, remove clams and shrimp with a slotted spoon and place into individually warmed bowls. Pour equal amounts of sauce over each.

This recipe is as easy as it looks. There are no tricks, just good common sense. Above all, use the freshest ingredients you can get.

STRACCIATELLA FLORENTINA

3 oz. spinach, cooked and chopped
6 cups chicken stock
4 eggs, beaten
2 T. Parmesan cheese

1. Heat the spinach in chicken stock. Bring to boil.
2. Stir in beaten eggs and Parmesan cheese. When eggs coagulate, serve immediately.

FETTUCINE ALFREDO

The better the egg noodle, the better the fettucine. If neither you nor your grandmother make your own, buy the best quality you can get.

1/2 lb. egg noodles
2 oz. butter
6 oz. cream (or half-and-half)
2 oz. Parmesan cheese, grated
Ground black pepper
1 oz. chicken stock

1. Bring lightly salted water to a boil. Add noodles and cook until slightly underdone.
2. In a separate pan, melt butter over moderate heat and add cream. Bring mixture to a low boil.
3. Drain noodles and add to butter/cream mixture. Mix well and cook for a few additional minutes.
4. Turn heat to low. Sprinkle cheese into mixture and fold gently until sauce starts to thicken. Add a few turns of pepper.
5. If mixture gets too thick, add chicken stock.
6. Serve on a warm platter. Add more cheese if desired, and an additional turn of pepper.

As sauce cools it will thicken and may turn pasty if too dry. On the other hand, too much chicken stock will make it runny, so be careful and use good judgment. A little practice will make you an expert.

INSALATA PRIMAVERA ALLA DORO'S

4 small heads Bibb lettuce cut into eighths
2 medium tomatoes
4 hearts of palm, cut into 1-inch pieces
4 artichoke hearts, halved
1 avocado, thinly sliced

DRESSING

2 cups salad oil
1 egg, beaten
2 T. white vinegar
3 drops Tabasco sauce
3 drops Lea & Perrins
1/2 t. mustard
Dash pepper
Shake or two of salt
Juice of 1/2 lemon

Beat oil gently with whisk and blend in all ingredients.

Continue whisking the dressing as you add ingredients or it may separate.

SCALLOPINI ALLA SORRENTINA

12 thin slices eggplant
10 oz. butter
Flour
12 slices thin, white veal
1 to 2 t. shallots (or green onions)
4 oz. white wine
6 oz. brown stock
4 oz. veal stock
12 thin slices prosciutto
12 thin slices mild cheese (Muenster, for example)
Parmesan cheese, grated
Parsley

1. Sauté eggplant in 2 oz. butter until light golden. Set aside.
2. Flour veal lightly. Place 4 oz. clarified butter in skillet and sauté veal quickly over medium heat, 1 minute on each side. Remove.
3. Pour all but a little butter from pan, add shallots and cook until they start to golden. Add white wine slowly. Add brown stock, and veal stock; when liquid starts to heat up add 4 oz. butter. Allow to thicken. Cook for 1 or 2 minutes. Remove from heat.
4. Top each piece of veal with one slice of eggplant, then one slice of prosciutto and one slice of mild cheese. Sprinkle Parmesan cheese over top.
5. Bake in hot oven for 2 minutes or place under broiler until cheese is melted and golden. Place veal on warm platter and cover with sauce. Sprinkle with fresh parsley and serve.

Don't forget to clarify the butter or it will burn. And don't get distracted while cooking the veal! It should be done very quickly.

CARCIOFINI DORATI

16 baby artichoke hearts, cut in half (top to bottom)
4 eggs, well beaten
Flour
Salt to taste
3 T. clarified butter (or 2 T. butter and 1 T. oil)
Parsley

1. Dip artichoke hearts in egg and pass through flour until
   well covered.
2. Heat clarified butter in pan. Sauté artichoke hearts quickly on all
   sides, about 1 to 2 minutes, and salt lightly. Remove from heat.
3. Drain the artichokes and garnish with parsley.

ZABAGLIONE ALLA DORO'S

4 egg yolks
2 oz. Marsala (or sweet sherry)
4 T. sugar
4 scoops vanilla ice cream
16 fresh strawberries

1. Combine egg yolks, wine and sugar and cook over low heat, stirring
   constantly.
2. Whip mixture until it thickens to whipped cream consistency.
3. Surround each scoop of ice cream with 4 strawberries and cover
   with Zabaglione Sauce.

***Over-cooking will produce sweet, wine-flavored scrambled eggs.
Pay attention!***

Giannutti's

Dinner for Four

Prosciutto and Melon

Sautéed Mussels

Salad Deluxe

Chicken alla Cacciatore

Baked Potatoes alla Siciliana

Farfalini

Wines:
With Mussels: Verdecchio

With Chicken: Chianti Brolio

Santo Cinquegrani, Owner

Anna Cimino, Head Chef

As a rule, family operated neighborhood restaurants do not receive much culinary notoriety, but Giannotti's is the exception. Situated in Forest Park, twenty minutes west of the Loop, Giannotti's reputation for serving superb Italian cuisine attracts a steady stream of Chicago residents despite its out-of-the-way location.

Although ownership of Giannotti's changed hands in 1976, few noticed any differences. "When the Giannottis decided to sell, we were prepared to maintain the same quality and standards that made the restaurant so successful," says Santo Cinquegrani, the new owner. "We kept the same menu, the same atmosphere and, most importantly, the same staff."

At the heart of that staff is chef Anna Cimino, who has been with Giannotti's since its opening day. Besides supervising the preparation of Giannotti's extensive regular menu, Anna seems to thrive on devising new dishes which are frequently offered as daily specials. Given sufficient time, requests for particular specialties are honored as well. "If we included Anna's entire repertoire," says Santo's daughter Sara, "we wouldn't have a menu, we'd have a book. This is a woman who genuinely loves to cook."

7711 Roosevelt Road, Forest Park

PROSCIUTTO AND MELON

1/2 honeydew melon
4 slices prosciutto

Cut honeydew into 4 pieces and wrap each with 1 slice of prosciutto.

SAUTÉED MUSSELS

2 lbs. California mussels
1/2 cup olive oil
1 cup white wine
1 t. red pepper seeds
2 T. chopped parsley

1. Carefully scour mussels under tap water to remove sand.
2. In a saucepan combine mussels, oil, wine, red pepper and
   1 T. parsley. Cover pan and cook over high flame for about
   15 minutes or until shells open.
3. Serve in opened shells with remaining parsley sprinkled on top.

***We use California mussels because they are bigger than the Boston
variety and easier to remove from their shells.***

SALAD DELUXE

1 head romaine lettuce, chopped
8 radishes, chopped
1 cucumber, diced
2 celery hearts, chopped
8 artichoke hearts
2 medium tomatoes, quartered
4 small pieces pickled cauliflower, chopped
1 small red onion, sliced
8 black olives
4 slices vinegared red peppers (rinsed, with seeds and stems removed)
Dressing

1. In a salad bowl combine the lettuce, radishes, cucumber, celery, and
   about half of the *Dressing*.
2. In another bowl, mix artichokes, tomatoes, cauliflower and
   remaining *Dressing*. Add these ingredients to those in
   the salad bowl.
3. Arrange onions, olives and peppers on top of the salad
   and serve.

DRESSING

1/2 cup olive oil
1/4 cup vinegar
Juice of 1/2 lemon
1/2 garlic clove, chopped
1/2 t. oregano
Salt and pepper to taste

Combine all ingredients and serve.

***Because of the fragile nature of some of the ingredients, we
mix the salad in two batches. For the same reason, we do not toss
the salad, but lay the *Dressing* over the vegetables and gently
mix them.***

CHICKEN ALLA CACCIATORE

2 whole fryers, cut into eighths
1/4 lb. butter
2 oz. olive oil
Salt and pepper to taste
1 oz. Cognac
1/2 cup fresh mushrooms, sliced
4 tomatoes, peeled
1 T. chopped parsley

1. Saute the chicken in butter and oil over a high flame until brown. Cover the skillet with foil, add salt and pepper, and put in 500 degree preheated oven. Bake for 7 to 8 minutes. Remove and keep warm.
2. In a saucepan, combine wine, Cognac and mushrooms. Allow the mixture to cook over medium heat until it has been reduced by half.
3. Add tomatoes and cook until mixture is creamy. Add parsley, pour over chicken and serve.

A good cook doesn't just use her eyes and her mouth, she also must use her head and her heart. Watch the food as it cooks. Taste it, of course, but be sensible and alert. Above all, enjoy what you're doing!

BAKED POTATOES ALLA SICILIANA

1 lb. potatoes, peeled and cut like French fries
4 T. butter
1/4 cup Romano cheese, grated
1/4 cup bread crumbs
1 T. parsley, chopped
1 clove garlic, chopped
Salt and pepper to taste

1. Bake the potatoes in the butter in a 400 degree preheated oven for about 20 minutes.
2. Combine the remaining ingredients.
3. When potatoes are done, sprinkle crumb mixture over the top and bake for an additional minute or until cheese has melted.

FARFALINI

3 eggs
1/4 t. baking soda
1/4 t. salt
1/4 t. corn oil
1/2 lb. flour
1 quart cooking oil
Powdered sugar

1. Mix the eggs, baking soda, salt, corn oil and flour to make a dough mixture; roll out until almost paper thin. Cut into 2x2 inch squares.
2. Pour cooking oil into a large saucepan and heat until very hot. Drop the squares of dough into oil and cook until lightly browned. Remove and drain. Allow to cool.
3. Sprinkle cookies with powdered sugar and serve.

greek islands

Dinner for Six

Taramosalata

Greek Salad

Greek Style Shrimp

Baked Okra

Galaktobouriko

Wine:
Corinth Dry, Boutari or Patraiki

Filandros Sguros, Gus Couchell, Paul Bournas, Owners
Filandros Sguros, Head Chef

Chicago has one of the largest Greek communities in the country, with the oldest concentration of its restaurants and businesses centered around Halsted Street and Jackson Boulevard in an area appropriately referred to as Greektown. Despite so much friendly competition nearby, the Greek Islands restaurant has managed to earn top culinary honors from both food critics and the dining public since it opened in 1971. "Taking nothing away from other Greek restaurants in the city," says Nick Sguros, the restaurant manager, "we feel we're the best because the owners themselves do all the cooking."

Owner-chef Filandros Sguros, Nick's father, has done little else, in fact, since his childhood in Greece. By 1964, his reputation was so widespread that he was asked to cook at the New York World's Fair. There Sguros' talents were noticed by a Greek restaurateur from Chicago who persuaded him to stay in the United States and head his kitchen staff. Seven years later, Sguros joined with four friends to open the Greek Islands. "From the start, all the recipes were original," says Nick. "My father brought them over from Greece in his head. They've been copied by just about everyone since."

766 W. Jackson Boulevard

TARAMOSALATA

1/4 lb. day-old firm-textured bread, crusts removed (about 4 slices)
1/3 cup water
1 3 1/2-oz. jar red caviar
2 t. grated onion
1/4 t. salt
2/3 cup vegetable oil
1/4 cup lemon juice
Greek olives
Lemon slices

1. Moisten bread with about 1/3 cup water.
2. Put bread, caviar, onion and salt in blender. Run on low speed and gradually and alternately add oil and lemon juice. (Do not let mixture get too thin; hold back on the oil if that appears to happen. This should be a fairly thick purée.)
3. Mound mixture on serving platter and chill.
4. Garnish with Greek olives and lemon slices. Serve with French or sourdough bread slices.

GREEK SALAD

2 heads lettuce
1 t. oregano
1 t. salt
1/2 cup olive oil
1/2 cup red wine vinegar
2 tomatoes, quartered
12 anchovy filets
1/4 lb. peppers toursi (pickled)
Greek olives
1/2 lb. feta cheese, cubed

1. After washing and drying lettuce, tear or shred it and place it in a large bowl.
2. Sprinkle lettuce with the oregano and salt, then add oil and vinegar. Toss thoroughly.
3. Add remaining vegetables and cheese to the top of the salad and serve.

GREEK STYLE SHRIMP

2 lbs. fresh shrimp
1 cup chopped green onions
1/2 cup oil
1 T. tomato paste
1 cup rosé wine
2 cups water
1 t. salt
1/2 t. pepper
1/2 lb. feta cheese, crumbled
2 tomatoes, peeled, seeded and chopped
1/2 cup chopped parsley

1. After washing shrimp, cook in boiling water until pink, about 5 minutes. Drain and arrange in large baking dish.
2. Sauté onions in the oil until tender. Stir in tomato paste and wine. Add the water, salt and pepper. Bring to boil, then reduce heat and simmer 5 to 10 minutes.
3. Sprinkle the cheese over the shrimp. Cover with the chopped tomatoes and parsley. Top with sauce.
4. Bake at 350 degrees for 30 minutes.

There are no tricks or secrets to these recipes. Sometimes it just takes patience to get a dish to turn out right. We've given out recipes before and people would sometimes complain that they tried them once and failed. We encourage them to try again, remembering what went wrong the first time, and make appropriate adjustments. Keep in mind that appliances, utensils, temperatures and even ingredients may vary, so your own good judgment is your best friend in the kitchen.

BAKED OKRA

3 lbs. fresh okra
1 cup red wine vinegar
1 cup chopped onions
2 cups oil
3 tomatoes, peeled, seeded and chopped
2 t. salt
1 t. pepper
1/2 cup chopped parsley

1. Place okra in a large saucepan. Pour in enough salted water to just cover the vegetable. Add the vinegar. Heat quickly and cook for just a minute or two. Do not boil; the okra should remain crisp. Drain okra and place in baking dish.
2. Sauté the onion in the oil until tender. Add tomatoes, salt, pepper and parsley and cook over moderate heat for 5 minutes.
3. Pour mixture over okra. Bake at 350 degrees for 45 minutes.

GALAKTOBOURIKO

We serve this custard dish hot with the syrup at room temperature, so it is necessary to make the syrup first in order to allow time for it to cool.

SYRUP

1 lb. sugar
4 cups water
1 stick cinnamon
6 cloves
1/2 lemon

1. Combine ingredients in a saucepan and heat to a boil. When it boils, test consistency by extracting a teaspoonful and checking to see if it's sticky and syrupy. If so, remove immediately. (Do not let mixture boil too long or the syrup will get too thick.)
2. Set aside and allow to cool at room temperature.

CUSTARD

1 quart milk
2 cups sugar
1 cup simigdali (available at many supermarkets and Greek groceries)
4 eggs
1/8 t. vanilla
1/4 lb. butter plus 4 T. melted butter
1 t. trimmed lemon peel
12 fillo leaves

1. Heat the milk and sugar in a saucepan. Bring to a boil.
2. In a separate saucepan, mix the simigdali, eggs and vanilla. Add the boiling milk and mix thoroughly. Bring combined mixture to a boil, them remove from heat. Add 1/4 lb. of butter and stir until it is melted. Add lemon peel.
3. Grease a small baking dish with butter. Take 2 sheets of fillo leaves and fold them in half. Lay them in bottom of pan so that half lie inside pan, half outside pan. Repeat procedure on all sides. Lay 1 additional leaf over bottom, covering overlapping fillo leaves.
4. Pour in custard mixture. Fold fillo flaps over the mixture and lay 2 additional leaves over top. Brush top with melted butter and bake at 250 degrees for 50 minutes.
5. When ready, glaze the top of the custard with the *Syrup*, cut into individual squares and serve.

NOTE: The *Syrup* recipe will produce much more quantity than you will need, but it is not possible to make it in smaller batches without losing some quality.

Jimmy's Place

Dinner for Six

Japanese-Style Marinated Salmon

Cold Spanish Gazpacho

Jimmy's Place Salad

Fresh Sea Scallops Yoshi Style

Caramel Apples with Rum and Ice Cream

Wines:
Pouilly-Fumé, Guenier Fils

Muscadet de Sèvre et Maine
Vouvray, M. Robin

Jimmy Rohr, Owner
Yoshi Katsumura, Chef

What's a nice restaurant like Jimmy's Place doing in an industrial area on Elston Avenue? The location was a deliberate choice by owner Jimmy Rohr in keeping with his practical, no-nonsense approach to running a restaurant. "People will go out of their way to dine in a good restaurant, particularly if they are guaranteed a parking space," says Rohr. "And there are literally hundreds of spots around here."

In an era of million dollar restaurant decor and mind-boggling glitz, Jimmy's Place offers a refreshing dose of unpretentiousness and charm. The small, forty-six seat room features a bright green, yellow and white color scheme, mirror-topped tables, chrome accessories and walls decorated with opera posters and programs. Along one wall of the narrow room, shoulder height windows permit a look into Rohr's immaculate, well-equipped kitchen.

Rohr describes his imaginative and frequently changing menu as International with French and Japanese overtones. "I am an American and my chef is Japanese which gives us a special blend of East and West and allows us the freedom to serve many types of food in a variety of ways. We're not locked into any one ethnic category." Rohr changes the menu monthly, offering seasonal specialties as they become available and various national dishes as the spirit moves him. The same menu may offer bouillabaisse, hasenpfeffer and Japanese-style marinated raw fish.

Chef Katsumura studied French cooking in Japan before coming to this country. In Chicago he began as a cook with the old Le Bastille and within six months was promoted to chef. Later he served as assistant chef with La Reserve where he caught the eye of Rohr, then managing the restaurant. "I knew he was good right away," says Rohr. "And I knew when I opened my own place I wanted him to head my kitchen staff."

3420 N. Elston

JAPANESE STYLE MARINATED SALMON

1 side fresh salmon
Pinch salt
2 cups dry white wine
2 cups white vinegar
2 bay leaves
1/2 t. whole black peppercorns
1 medium onion, sliced
2 carrots, sliced
1 large head leaf lettuce
6 tomato wedges
6 lemon wedges
1 jar capers
Parsley sprigs

1. Sprinkle salmon with salt, then carefully debone, leaving the skin intact. Refrigerate salmon for 1/2 day.
2. Combine the wine, vinegar, bay leaves, peppercorns, onions and carrots. Pour into shallow pan and add salmon. Marinate in the liquid 1/2 hour on each side. Remove from marinade and towel dry. Save onions and carrots for garnish.
3. Clean the lettuce, drain and arrange on individual plates.
4. Slice salmon lengthwise in very thin slices. Arrange on top of lettuce and garnish with onions and carrots. Decorate plates with tomato wedges, lemon wedges, capers and parsley sprigs.

Be sure to get the freshest salmon available; anything else will have disappointing results.

COLD SPANISH GAZPACHO

1 quart tomato juice
1 lemon
2 medium green peppers, seeded and diced finely
1 small onion, diced
2 ripe tomatoes, peeled, seeded and diced
1 small cucumber, seeded and diced
3 small cloves garlic, minced
Salt to taste
Tabasco sauce to taste
2 T. olive oil

1. Pour tomato juice in a bowl and add the juice of one lemon.
   Mix well.
2. Add all other ingredients, mix well and serve.

NOTE: If the soup is too thick you may add cold water to it.

JIMMY'S PLACE SALAD

2 bunches fresh spinach
1 head iceberg lettuce
1 head Boston lettuce
1 head romaine lettuce
1 package enoki (Japanese mushrooms) or 1 package fresh
    mushrooms, sliced
12 tomato wedges
6 slices bacon, cubed and fried crisp
Croutons
6 lemon wedges
6 radishes, sliced
Dressing

1. Wash and dry spinach and lettuce separately. Break all lettuce into
   bite-size pieces and put in mixing bowl. Pour half of the lemon
   Dressing over and mix well. Arrange lettuce neatly on
   individual plates.
2. Break spinach leaves and mix with remaining *Dressing*. Arrange
   on top of lettuce on plates.
3. Garnish plate with mushrooms, tomato wedges and lemon wedges.
   Sprinkle with bacon bits, croutons and radishes.

DRESSING

1/4 cup fresh lemon juice
1/4 cup Dijon mustard
Dash salt
Dash white pepper
1 1/2 cups vegetable oil

1. Combine lemon juice, mustard, salt and white pepper in a blender. Mix well.
2. While blender is running, slowly add oil. Refrigerate.

FRESH SEA SCALLOPS YOSHI STYLE

You may substitute frozen store-bought pastry for the homemade recipe given here, but you will sacrifice something in taste and flakiness. It is not difficult to make, but it is time consuming, so time consuming, in fact, that we're one of only a very few restaurants in Chicago that makes its own. If you do have the time, though, it's well worth the effort.

NOTE: This dough should be made a day in advance to give sufficient time for remaining preparation.

PUFF PASTRY

1 lb. butter (very soft)
1 lb. flour
1 cup water
Dash salt
1 egg for egg wash

1. Combine 1/4 lb. butter, flour, water and salt in a blender and mix
   well until dough does not stick to your fingers when touched.
   Remove to a bowl and refrigerate for 2 hours.
2. Roll dough out on a floured board. In center of dough spread
   remaining soft butter, then fold edges of dough over butter,
   covering it completely. Refrigerate for 1 hour.
3. Remove dough from refrigerator and let sit for 1/2 hour. Roll out
   dough lengthwise, roughly the shape of a business letter, and fold
   it in three, also like a letter. Refrigerate and cover with a wet
   towel for 1 hour.
4. Repeat above process, folding dough in four.
5. Repeat process, folding dough in three.
6. Repeat process, folding dough in four. After refrigeration, the
   dough is ready to be used.
7. On a floured board, roll out the dough to a thickness of
   1/4 to 1/3 inch and cut into 3x5 inch rectangles. Water edges of
   the rectangles and with some extra dough make 1/2 inch strips to
   lay around the sides. Press down strips lightly with a fork. Brush
   rectangle with an egg wash with a drop of water. Bake at 375
   degrees for 10 to 15 minutes or until golden. Keep warm.

Scallop Preparation—

2 cups cooked spinach
6 small potatoes, peeled
1 white leek
1 small carrot
1 celery stalk
1 quart white wine
3 shallots, minced
3 sticks butter, very soft
Juice from 1/2 lemon
Salt to taste
Cayenne pepper to taste
1 cup milk
2 quarts water
1/2 t. salt
Dash white pepper
3 lbs. fresh sea scallops
Chopped parsley

1. Sauté spinach in butter, season to taste and keep warm.
2. Boil potatoes in salted water. Keep warm.
3. Julienne the leek, carrot and celery. Cook in salted water for
   3 minutes. Keep warm.
4. In a large saucepan, heat the wine and shallots. Reduce mixture
   until liquid barely covers bottom of pan. Slowly, using a wire
   whisk, add the butter, beating constantly. Add the lemon juice,
   salt and cayenne pepper. Keep mixture warm.
5. In a large saucepan, combine milk, water, salt and white pepper
   and bring to a boil. As soon as boiling point is reached, add
   scallops and cook until liquid returns to a boil *plus 1 minute.*
   Remove and drain scallops.
6. Put puff pastry on plate, cover with bed of spinach, top with
   scallops and julienned vegetables and cover with sauce. Sprinkle
   with parsley and add potato on side. Serve immediately.

CARAMEL APPLES WITH RUM AND ICE CREAM

1 1/2 sticks sweet butter
1 1/3 cups sugar
1 t. lemon juice
4 apples, peeled, cored and sliced thin
1 1/2 T. dark rum
12 scoops coffee ice cream

1. Melt butter in skillet and add sugar and lemon juice. Cook over medium heat until sugar turns to a light brown caramel.
2. Add apple slices and cook 2 to 3 minutes.
3. Add rum and serve immediately over ice cream scoops.

Le Perroquet

Dinner for Four to Six

Mushroom Mousse

Aubergines au Gratin

Pickled Beef Tongue with Lobster and Green Peppercorns

Blueberry Soufflé

Wines:
With Mousse: Riesling, Alsatian
With Tongue: Fumé Blanc, Robert Mondavi

Jovan Trboyevic, Owner

Even your entrance into Le Perroquet is special; a tiny Left Bank-like elevator lifts you three stories above Walton Street and opens onto a world of understated elegance and extraordinary cuisine. Owner Jovan Trboyevic has finely honed his restaurant down to the last detail, making it one of the finest in America.

Since its opening in 1972, Trboyevic has shifted Le Perroquet's menu away from classic French cuisine and toward la nouvelle cuisine—the starchless, low fat cooking style developed by the young ex-pâtissier, Michel Guérard. Trboyevic's reasons for doing so were twofold: "For one thing, most Americans had not yet been exposed to it, so I saw the opportunity to pioneer this sophisticated new form of French cooking in the Midwest. I also felt that today's weight conscious public wanted to be able to enjoy haute cuisine without worrying about the effect heavy, rich sauces would have on their waistlines." The result is exquisite, yet delicate food, prepared and served with the kind of professional dedication often attempted but seldom accomplished.

"Actually, Le Perroquet has no 'executive chef' per se. Our kitchen staff is made up of a group of young men who work together on an equal basis preparing our menu," explains Trboyevic. "It would be unfair to single out one among them for particular honors. They all do a superb job."

70 E. Walton Street

MUSHROOM MOUSSE

This recipe calls for the use of duxelles which are not difficult to make, but are time consuming, so prepare them in advance.

DUXELLES

1/4 lb. butter
1 lb. mushrooms, finely chopped
1 T. shallots, chopped
1 T. lemon juice
Salt to taste

Heat butter in a heavy skillet. Add mushrooms, shallots and lemon juice and cook on low heat until all the liquid has evaporated and the mushrooms are dark and dry. (This may take an hour or more.) Season lightly with salt.

MOUSSE

1 T. butter
1 T. flour
1/3 cup milk
Salt and pepper to taste
Touch of nutmeg
Duxelles
3 eggs, separated

1. Melt the butter in a small, heavy saucepan. Stir in flour and cook, stirring, until golden and bubbling.
2. Mix in milk and cook over medium heat, stirring, until thick. Season with salt, pepper and the nutmeg.
3. Add the *Duxelles* and mix well. Stir in three egg yolks, then remove the mixture from heat and allow to cool slightly.
4. Beat the egg whites until they are stiff. Fold into *Duxelle* mixture.
5. Heavily butter a 5-cup ring mold. Pour *Mousse* into the mold and place it in a roasting pan. Pour hot water 2/3 of the way up the mold and bake in a 375 degree even for 25 minutes. Allow to cool 5 minutes before unmolding.
6. Cover *Mousse* with *Sauce Supreme.*

SAUCE SUPREME

4 T. butter
4 T. flour
2 cups chicken stock
Salt and pepper to taste
Dash lemon juice
3/4 cup heavy cream
1 to 2 T. black truffles, finely julienned

1. Melt butter in a heavy saucepan, blend in flour and cook until
   golden, stirring.
2. Gradually stir in chicken stock and cook, stirring, until thickened.
   Season with salt, pepper and lemon juice.
3. Mix in heavy cream and truffles and heat, but do not boil.

***The recipes included here reflect a more classical approach to French
cooking. La nouvelle cuisine requires intricate preparation and considerable
experience to do properly and since few home cooks have the right
equipment or enough patience to achieve the proper effect, we feel
there is a greater chance for success with these dishes. Don't get lazy,
though; they're quite challenging in their own right!***

AUBERGINES AU GRATIN

Tomato Topping
1 1 1/2-lb. eggplant
Hollandaise Sauce
Sauce Supreme II
Cream Glaze

TOMATO TOPPING

This could be prepared a day in advance.

1 large garlic clove, peeled and crushed
1/2 t. coarse (kosher) salt
3 T. olive oil
1 medium onion, peeled and minced
1 1-lb. 12-oz. can Italian plum tomatoes,
   drained and coarsely chopped
2 bay leaves
1 t. thyme
1 T. tomato paste

1. Mash the garlic to the consistency of a paste. Stir in salt,
   then set aside.
2. Heat oil in a 10-inch skillet. Add onion and cook over low heat,
   stirring constantly, for 3 minutes or until onion is soft but not
   brown. Stir in garlic paste and cook 1 to 2 minutes longer.
3. Add tomatoes, bay leaves, thyme and tomato paste. Cook over
   medium heat, stirring frequently, for about 20 minutes or until
   all excess liquid is evaporated and tomatoes are thick.
4. Correct seasoning, remove bay leaves and set aside.

NOTE: If the *Tomato Topping* is prepared in advance, reheat
        thoroughly before assembling with eggplant.

Eggplant preparation—

1 1 1/2-lb. eggplant
2 cups olive oil
Salt and pepper to taste

1. Cut each end of the eggplant blunt. Remove all skin with a vegetable peeler. Cut crosswise into 6 1/2-inch thick rounds.
2. Heat oil in a 9-inch skillet to 225 to 250 degrees. Add eggplant slices 3 at a time and cook, shaking the skillet gently to baste the top of each slice with oil, about 3 minutes or just until a paring knife inserted into the eggplant slices meets no resistance.
3. Remove and press eggplant slices carefully between double thicknesses of paper towels to remove excess oil. Season with salt and pepper.

NOTE: The eggplant may be prepared as much as two hours in advance. Should this be the case, allow the eggplant slices to cool after frying, wrap them and set aside at room temperature. When ready to use, reheat quickly in several tablespoons of oil and blot with paper towels.

HOLLANDAISE SAUCE

2 large egg yolks
1 T. warm water
1/2 cup hot clarified butter

1. Place egg yolks and water in the top of a double boiler. Set over simmering water and whisk 30 seconds to heat.
2. Slowly add butter in a thin, steady stream, whisking vigorously until sauce is thick and foamy.
3. Set aside covered with a sheet of plastic wrap touching the top of the sauce.

SAUCE SUPREME II

24 oz. clear chicken stock
3 cups whipping cream
1/2 lb. very white, firm mushrooms with closed gills, wiped clean
1/4 t. coarse (kosher) salt
White pepper, freshly ground
Dash Tabasco sauce

1. Place chicken stock in a 10-inch skillet and simmer until reduced to 1 pint. Set aside to cool.
2. Place whipping cream in a 10- or 11-inch skillet. Remove the stems from the mushrooms and add all the stems to the cream. Halve 2 oz. of the whitest mushroom caps and add to cream. Cook over low heat about 35 minutes, stirring occasionally. Lower heat and simmer, stirring frequently to ensure that the mixture does not scorch, until cream is thick and reduced about one-half (15 to 20 minutes longer).
3. Strain cream through a double mesh strainer (chinois) or through a strainer lined with a double thickness of cheesecloth. Press mushrooms firmly to extract all liquid.
4. Mix reduced stock with all the strained cream in a 10- or 11-inch skillet. Add salt, several grinds white pepper and Tabasco sauce. Simmer over medium heat 30 to 40 minutes, stirring frequently, or until sauce is reduced to about 1 3/4 cups.
5. Strain in a double meshed sieve or through a cheesecloth-lined strainer. Agitate but do not press the residue that remains in strainer. Discard residue. Cover sauce with a sheet of plastic wrap until just before serving.

CREAM GLAZE

1/3 cup *Sauce Supreme II*
1/4 cup *Hollandaise Sauce*
3 T. Parmesan cheese
Pinch salt
White pepper, freshly ground
Dash Tabasco
1 cup whipping cream, beaten to firm peaks

Place *Sauce Supreme II, Hollandaise,* cheese, salt, several grinds of pepper and Tabasco in a large bowl. Carefully, but thoroughly, fold in the whipped cream. Cover and chill until ready to use.

Final assembly—

1. Preheat broiler on high and adjust oven rack to within 2 inches of the heat source.
2. Place each hot eggplant slice on an individual ovenproof serving dish. Sprinkle lightly with salt and pepper.
3. Spoon 3 T. hot *Tomato Topping* onto each eggplant slice. Top with 1/4 cup *Cream Glaze* placed directly on the *Tomato Topping.*
4. Place plates under broiler just until the glaze melts and browns lightly. Serve immediately.

Be sure that both the eggplant and *Tomato Topping* are very hot before assembling.

PICKLED BEEF TONGUE WITH LOBSTER AND GREEN PEPPERCORNS

3 to 4 lb. raw pickled beef tongue
2 1 1/4- to 1 1/2-lb. live lobsters
Lobster Sauce
Lobster Garnish
Lobster Sabayon Sauce
Peppercorn/Pear Garnish

Tongue preparation—

3 1/2 to 4 quarts cold water
6 whole peppercorns
2 bay leaves, crushed

1. Place tongue in a 6 quart soup kettle or dutch oven. Cover with water and add peppercorns and bay leaves. Cover and bring to a bubble. Remove any scum that rises. Set cover slightly ajar and cook at a rapid simmer for about 3 hours or until juices run

clear when pierced. Uncover and cool tongue in its cooking liquid.
2. When cool, remove skin. Trim off the small bones and all the
   fibrous material at the thick end. Trim along the curve to
   remove additional tough matter.
3. Return tongue to cooking liquid. Cover loosely. Just before
   serving, reheat tongue thoroughly and cut into 24 thin slices.

Lobster preparation—

1. Firmly grasp the back of the lobster and place it on a carving board.
   Place a dish towel over the head and claws and with a chef's knife or
   cleaver, cut off the tail as quickly and as close to the body as
   possible. Set tail aside.
2. Holding the lobster by the body with the head facing you, twist off
   each claw. Use the backside of the knife to crack the light colored
   underside of each claw with one gentle but firm thwack. Grasp the
   large part of the claw with one end of the towel and the spiny
   connecting joint with the other end. Twist to free claw from joint
   and repeat with second claw. Set claws and joint aside.
3. Turn the lobster on its back and split the body in half lengthwise.
   Scrape out the soft greenish matter (coral) with a spoon and set it
   aside in a small bowl. If there is any red matter (roe) add it to the
   bowl. Pull out and discard the fibrous pouch underneath the eyes.
4. Cut the body into 4 pieces, then twist off the legs and break each
   in half. Set all pieces of the body and legs aside with other parts
   of the lobster until ready to cook the *Lobster Sauce.*

NOTE: If you are squeamish about cutting up a live lobster, you may
       either have it cut up for you (use only the most reputable
       seafood establishment; lobster meat can spoil quickly and
       must be as fresh as possible), or you may drop the lobster in
       boiling water for about a minute before beginning. Be sure
       to place it head first, upside down in the water for the quickest
       and most humane results. Remove it when limp and proceed
       with the cutting.

LOBSTER SAUCE

1/4 cup clarified butter
1 medium onion, peeled and sliced
6 medium shallots, peeled and sliced
1 medium garlic clove, crushed
2 medium carrots, peeled and sliced
3 celery ribs, leaves removed, sliced
2 lobsters, cut up
1/3 cup cognac or brandy
2/3 cup dry white wine
1/3 cup Madeira
4 ripe medium tomatoes, cored and chopped
1/3 cup chopped parsley
2 bay leaves
1/2 t. dried or 1 t. fresh thyme leaves
1 T. dried or 2 T. fresh tarragon leaves
Pinch salt
Pepper to taste
2 T. tomato paste
Dash Tabasco sauce
2 1/2 cups fish stock or water
1/3 cup whipping cream

1. Place the butter in an 11- or 12-inch skillet. Add onion, shallots, garlic, carrots and celery and sauté over high heat for about 3 minutes or until soft.
2. Turn heat to medium and add all lobster pieces, including tails, claws, coral and roe. Heat and ignite brandy, pour over lobster and allow to flame.
3. Add wine, Madeira, tomatoes, parsley, bay leaves, thyme, tarragon, salt, pepper, tomato paste, Tabasco and about 1 cup of the fish stock (or water) so that the liquid covers the lobster pieces by at least half. Remove lobster tails, extract meat, break up and return shells to skillet. (Preserve and chill lobster meat.)
4. Simmer sauce rapidly for 4 to 5 minutes, then remove claws and set aside to cool. Use back of a wooden spoon to break up large pieces of shell remaining in sauce. Simmer 15 minutes longer, again break up the shells, then add 1 additional cup of stock. Turn heat to low and simmer slowly for about 20 minutes.
5. Add remaining broth and simmer 5 to 10 minutes longer or until

sauce measures 1 1/2 cups after straining through a fine-meshed sieve or strainer. (Be sure to extract liquid from shells and vegetables by exerting firm pressure on them when straining.) Discard vegetables and shells. Skim the strained liquid of any fat and stir in the whipping cream.

6. Transfer the mixture to a large saucepan and simmer over medium heat until it is reduced to between 2/3 to 3/4 cup. Set aside.

LOBSTER GARNISH

This must be prepared just before serving.

2 reserved lobster tails
4 reserved lobster claws
2 T. clarified butter
2 T. Cognac or brandy

1. Halve tail meat lengthwise and remove intestine. Slice each half of the tail crosswise into 5 small cubes. Set aside.
2. Use kitchen shears to cut away claw shell. Carefully slip out the whole claw meat.
3. Heat butter in an 8- or 9-inch skillet. Add lobster tail pieces and toss over high heat for about 45 seconds. Add claw meat and cook just long enough to heat through.
4. Turn heat off, add brandy and flame. Pour off juices into strained lobster liquid, then cover tail and claw meat with foil to keep warm.

LOBSTER SABAYON SAUCE
and PEPPERCORN/PEAR GARNISH

3 large egg yolks
3 T. white wine
1 t. tarragon wine vinegar
1 1/2 cups strained *Lobster Sauce*
2 T. green peppercorns, rinsed and patted dry
2 pears, peeled and sliced for garnish

1. Place egg yolks, wine and vinegar in the top of a double boiler.
   Set over simmering water and whisk 30 seconds to heat.
2. Slowly add *Lobster Sauce* in a thin, steady stream, whisking
   vigorously until thick, foamy and very hot. Adjust seasoning.

Final assembly—

Place 4 hot tongue slices on each serving plate. Sauce lightly and top
with lobster pieces and/or a claw. Sprinkle a few green peppercorns
over each plate and arrange pears neatly at the side. Serve
immediately.

BLUEBERRY SOUFFLÉ

1 3/4 cup fresh or thawed frozen blueberries
1/2 cup sugar
2 t. butter, to coat soufflé dish
3 T. sugar, to coat soufflé dish
4 large egg whites
Pinch cream of tartar (optional)
Powdered sugar

1. In a food processor or blender, purée the blueberries for about
   20 seconds. With the machine on, pour 1/4 cup sugar into purée
   and mix 5 seconds longer.
2. Transfer the mixture to a 2-quart saucepan and cook over medium
   heat, stirring constantly, 4 to 5 minutes or until the mixture is
   dark, shiny and even colored and measures 1 cup. Cool mixture at
   least 15 minutes.
3. Coat a 1-quart (4-cup) soufflé dish generously with butter. Add
   3 T. sugar and turn dish until sugar clings evenly over bottom
   and sides. Tap out excess. Set dish aside.
4. Preheat oven to 450 degrees, adjust rack to bottom. Prepare a
   water bath into which the soufflé dish will sit without floating—
   an 8x8x1 1/2-inch glass baking dish is ideal. Fill dish with about
   1 inch of cold water and place it in the oven.
5. In a clean, dry electric mixer or copper bowl, beat egg whites
   until foamy. (If bowl is not copper, add cream of tartar at this
   point.) Beat whites to soft peaks, then begin to add remaining
   sugar gradually. Do not beat whites to firm peaks. As soon as the
   sugar is added, fold the blueberry mixture thoroughly into the egg
   whites. Pour mixture into the prepared souffle dish and use a cake
   icing spatula to scrape the mixture absolutely level with the top
   of the soufflé dish. Carefully clean off the rim and sides of the
   dish. Bake 20 to 25 minutes until puffy and browned. Remove
   dish from oven and sprinkle immediately with powdered sugar.

NOTE: To freeze fresh blueberries in season, pour them onto
       a cookie sheet with sides. Freeze them for about two hours,
       then pack them in plastic bags and freeze until ready to use.
       Thaw them in a mixing bowl in the refrigerator.

Maxim's
de Paris

Dinner for Four

Billi Bi
(Cream of Mussels)

Sole Albert

Veal Orloff

Maxim's Salad

Crêpes Veuve Joyeuse
(French Crêpes Filled with Lemon Soufflé)

Wines:
Corton-Charlemagne, Joseph Drouhin, 1976

Château Montrose, 1970

With Dessert: Château La Tour Blanche, 1972

Nancy Goldberg, Owner
Jean-Marie Martel, Executive Chef

In December, 1963 a bit more glitter was added to Chicago's already sparkling Gold Coast. In something of a culinary coup, the owner of Maxim's de Paris, one of the world's most famous restaurants, agreed to sanction the opening of a restaurant in Chicago bearing the Maxim's name, to date the only one of its kind in the United States.

The original Maxim's in Paris opened in 1893 during a period often referred to as La Belle Epoque. It was, and is, so immensely popular that the French government has declared Maxim's an historical monument and has forbidden any alteration of its 1900 decor. The Chicago counterpart is an exact replica of that French treasure, complete with the same rose silk shaded table lamps, red velvet seats and banquettes, mahogany walls, massive cut glass mirrors and rococo paintings.

Owner Nancy Goldberg seems intent on preserving the rich history and traditions of Maxim's in spite of a world full of variables. "In the fifteen years we've been here, so much has changed—the whole social structure, in fact—but we have stayed the same. We offer the same quality, the same service and the same decor. Maxim's in Paris has been successful doing the same thing for eighty-five years; we think there is a good chance we'll be around for at least another seventy years, too."

Executive Chef Jean-Marie Martel started cooking in his father's restaurant in Lille, France. Eventually traveling to England, he worked in both the Savoy and Claridge's in London before coming to the United States. In 1976 he joined the staff of Maxim's and recently rose to the position of Executive Chef.

1300 N. Astor

BILLI BI

***Many of our dishes, including this one, duplicate the original
Maxim's recipes exactly. We pride ourselves on maintaining a classical
French tradition.***

1 lb. mussels, shelled and cleaned
1/3 cup dry white wine
1 onion, sliced
2/3 cup water
1 bouquet garni (thyme, bay leaf, celery)
Salt and pepper to taste
1 pint whipping cream
1 t. arrowroot

1. Put mussels, wine, onion, water, bouquet garni, salt and pepper in
   saucepan and cover. Cook for 10 minutes on low heat.
2. Strain the mussels. Return to liquid *and* heat.
3. Reduce the liquid to 2/3 of the original and add the whipping cream.
   Bring to a boil and then simmer for 10 minutes.
4. Moisten the arrowroot with a little water and add to the mixture.
   Pour over mussels.

NOTE: This may be served hot or cold.

SOLE ALBERT

Many of Maxim's dishes are named after early chefs and patrons. Albert was an early chef and this recipe was his invention.

4 12-oz. filets of sole
5 oz. clarified butter
1/2 lb. fresh white breadcrumbs
1/2 cup water
Sauce Albert

1. Place the filets of sole in a pan with the butter and breadcrumbs on the top and brown them under the broiler.
2. Add the water and bake at 350 degrees for 10 minutes. Remove the filets and keep warm. Save pan liquid for sauce.
3. To serve, put the *Sauce Albert* on a platter and set sole on top.

SAUCE ALBERT

1 lb. butter, softened
1 oz. shallots, chopped
1 cup vermouth
1/2 cup white wine
1 T. beef glaze
Salt and pepper to taste
2 t. lobster, diced

1. To the liquid left in the baking pan add the shallots, vermouth, white wine, and beef glaze. Reduce until almost dry.
2. Beat the butter and add it with the salt and pepper to the reduced sauce. Strain.
3. Add the lobster and sauté it briefly in the butter.

Like all good recipes, this takes practice. A good cook must gain the experience to know from the look, taste and smells of food whether or not adjustments are necessary.

VEAL ORLOFF

This is a complicated recipe and it is most important to read the instructions completely before beginning.

4 medallions of veal (6 oz. each)
2 oz. butter
1 truffle
Mornay Sauce
Madeira Sauce
Duxelles
White Sauce

1. Sauté the veal in the butter for about 7 minutes. Set aside and keep warm on a tray.
2. When ready to serve, put 1 T. of the *Duxelles* on top of each medallion. Cover with the *Mornay Sauce* and glaze under the broiler.
3. Put a slice of truffle on top and serve with *Madeira Sauce* on the side.

MORNAY SAUCE

4 T. *White Sauce*
1 egg yolk
2 oz. Parmesan cheese, grated
2 T. whipping cream
Salt and pepper to taste

1. Combine *White Sauce*, egg yolk and Parmesan cheese and cook 3 minutes, stirring.
2. Remove mixture from stove and add whipping cream, salt and pepper.

DUXELLES

1/2 small onion, chopped
2 oz. butter
1/2 lb. fresh mushrooms, chopped
Salt and pepper to taste

1. Sauté the onions in butter until the liquid is cooked out.
2. Add the mushrooms, salt and pepper and cook for 15 minutes. Make sure all the liquid is cooked off.

MADEIRA SAUCE

1/2 cup Madeira
4 large mushrooms, diced
3 T. veal stock
2 oz. butter
Salt and pepper to taste

1. After cooking the medallions, deglaze the pan with the Madeira.
2. Add the mushrooms and reduce.
3. Add veal stock and cook for 5 minutes.
4. Add butter, salt and pepper and strain.

WHITE SAUCE

2 T. butter
1 to 1 1/2 T. flour
1 cup milk
1 small onion, chopped
1 carrot, chopped
Salt and pepper to taste

1. Melt the butter in a saucepan and add the flour slowly.
2. Stir in the milk and add the onion, carrot, salt and pepper. Add
   more flour if necessary to achieve sauce consistency.
3. Strain the sauce.

MAXIM'S SALAD

Bibb lettuce
Avocado, sliced
Tomatoes, quartered
Hearts of palm
Artichoke hearts or bottoms

DRESSING

3 T. oil
2 T. white vinegar
1 t. Dijon mustard
Salt and pepper to taste

Mix all ingredients well and pour over salad.

CRÊPES VEUVE JOYEUSE

1 T. flour
2 eggs
2 t. sugar
1 cup milk
2 oz. melted butter

1. Mix the flour, eggs, sugar and milk and beat. Add the melted
   butter and strain.
2. Pour about 2 T. batter into a hot greased skillet and cook crêpes for
   1 to 3 minutes on each side.

FILLING

2 t. flour
2 t. sugar
2 egg yolks
1 cup milk
Zest of 1 lemon and juice
4 egg whites, beaten

1. Mix the flour, sugar and egg yolks. Heat the milk and add. Cook
   until mixture begins to thicken, then add the lemon zest and juice
   and cook for 2 minutes.
2. Add the beaten egg whites and fold in with spatula.
3. Butter an oven-proof tray from which crêpes may be served directly
   and place crêpes on it. Fill each one with *Soufflé Filling* and fold
   in half. Cook at 350 degrees for 18 minutes. Serve immediately.

MIOMIR'S SERBIAN CLUB

Dinner for Six

Corba
(Serbian Beef and Vegetable Soup)

Royal Moussaka

Lovacka Snicla
(Huntsman's Schnitzel)

Apple Strudel

Wine:
Rajnski Rizling, Zilavka, or Prokupac

Miomir Radovanovic, Owner
Cveta Zugic, Head Chef

When you enter Miomir's Serbian Club, chances are you'll be given a warm and enthusiastic welcome by the ebullient owner, Miomir Radovanovic, whose energy level seems high enough to power a small Serbian village. Miomir seems to be everywhere: table hopping, chatting with old friends and making newcomers feel at home. "I want people to think of this as their second home," says Miomir. "They should sit where they want, eat what they want and drink what they want. Their pleasure is my greatest pleasure."

A journalist in his native Yugoslavia, Miomir couldn't live under the restrictive pressures put on him by the post-war Communist regime and he escaped to France. He later emigrated to the United States and in 1971 opened Miomir's. "Because Yugoslavia is a country between the East and West, it offers dishes that are a combination of the best of both worlds," Miomir explains. "The uninitiated will find the food less spicy than Middle Eastern cuisine and a little more spicy than German or Hungarian fare."

Head Chef Cveta Zugic is Yugoslavian born and has been with Miomir's since 1972.

2255 W. Lawrence Avenue

CŎRBA

In Yugoslavia, celebrations can go on for days. Enormous amounts of food are prepared—suckling pig, lamb, stuffed cabbage and so on—but traditionally, all feasts begin with *cŏrba*.

1 lb. veal on bone
1 lb. short ribs
1 lb. beef bones
Salt and pepper to taste
3 onions, chopped
2 cups carrots, chopped
2 cups celery, chopped
2 cups parsley and root, chopped
2 cups parsnips, chopped
1 cup red or green peppers, chopped
1 gallon cold water
3 T. beef baste
2 T. flour
1/4 cup oil
1 T. paprika

1. Place all vegetables, beef and seasonings in a large soup pot. Be sure to put beef on bottom.
2. Add 1 gallon of cold water. Cook on low heat 2 1/2 hours.
3. Remove beef and bones. Scrape off meat from bones and return to soup. Discard bones. Add beef baste.
4. In a saucepan, combine the flour and oil over medium heat. Remove from heat and stir in paprika. Add mixture to *cŏrba* and allow soup to boil. Remove from heat and serve immediately.

Like most good soups, the bones are the most important ingredient—the more bones, the richer the flavor.

ROYAL MOUSSAKA

4 medium eggplants, peeled and cut lengthwise
Flour
6 eggs, beaten
Oil
2 onions, chopped
1 lb. ground veal
1 lb. ground beef
Salt and pepper to taste
1 quart milk
Sour cream

1. Dip each eggplant piece in flour, then into 2 beaten eggs, then again
   into flour.
2. Heat some oil in a skillet, and sauté eggplant until golden brown;
   set aside.
3. In a large skillet, sauté onions, meat, salt and pepper until browned.
4. Grease a large casserole dish and place a layer of eggplant on
   bottom. Cover with some meat mixture and continue layering,
   making sure last layer is eggplant.
5. Mix remaining eggs with the milk and season with salt. Pour
   mixture over casserole of eggplant and meat until it
   covers completely.
6. Bake at 350 degrees for about 1 1/2 hours or until golden brown.
   Serve with sour cream.

***Moussaka was originally a Greek dish made with lamb. Serbians
use beef and veal and make a much milder version.***

APPLE STRUDEL

1 package fillo leaves
3 T. melted butter
6 to 8 sour apples, peeled and thinly sliced
1 cup sugar
2 t. ground cinnamon
Powdered sugar

1. Carefully remove fillo leaves from package and unfold. Cover with a plastic sheet.
2. Place one leaf on a greased cookie sheet and brush lightly with melted butter. Place second leaf on top of first and repeat process until 3 leaves have been buttered.
3. Put apples in a strip on edge of dough nearest you, leaving about a 1-inch border. Sprinkle apples with sugar and cinnamon. Roll as for a jellyroll. Brush top with melted butter.
4. Bake at 350 degrees for about 35 to 40 minutes or until light brown. Sprinkle with powdered sugar. Cut in 3-inch sections and serve.

Nick's Fishmarket

Dinner for Six

Orange Russian Cocktail

Crab Legs à la Marcus

Greek Salad

Steak Soup

Fishmarket Catfish

Zucchini Almandine

Papaya Gerald

Wines:
Sauvignon Blanc, Sterling
Pinot Chardonnay, Geyser Peak
With Dessert: Dom Perignon, Möet et Chandon, 1970

Nick Nickolas and Jeff Harman, Owners
Robert Ricci, Executive Chef

Although Nick's Fishmarket opened in the First National Plaza such a short time ago, the excellence of food and service that made the Waikiki and Beverly Hills branches so successful has quickly established it as one of the most popular restaurants in Chicago.

Owner Nick Nickolas attributes no mystery to the restaurant's appeal. "Food is a simple thing, really. If you prepare it honestly, consistently and with quality you will be successful. Caring is the key. I care about our food and the people who come here to eat it."

With over sixty seafood items on the menu, even the most demanding visitor should find something to suit his taste. Nickolas, who spent several years in Hawaii after a stint as a linebacker with his hometown Oakland Raiders, flies in fresh Hawaiian fish, such as Mahi Mahi and Ulua and other seldom-seen seafood items, several times a week.

Executive Chef Robert Ricci started his professional cooking career with the original Nick's Fishmarket in Waikiki and since 1969 has worked in all of them.

One First National Plaza

ORANGE RUSSIAN COCKTAIL

Frozen Strolichnaya vodka
1 large orange

Fill a 32-oz. brandy snifter 3/4 full of ice. Pour 3 or 4 shots of vodka over ice and garnish with large pieces of orange rind.

CRAB LEGS À LA MARCUS

12 large Alaskan king crab legs, shelled
Water
Garlic Butter

Simmer crab legs in 1/2 inch water for about 5 minutes; drain and cover with *Garlic Butter.*

GARLIC BUTTER

1/2 lb. soft butter
1/2 bunch parsley sprigs, finely chopped
1/2 oz. brandy
1 oz. white wine
2 dashes Tabasco sauce
2 dashes angostura bitters
2 dashes Worcestershire sauce
2 cloves garlic, finely chopped

Combine all ingredients and simmer very slowly for a few minutes.

It is very important not to brown the butter or garlic. Cook it very slowly over a very low heat.

This same *Garlic Butter* can be used with escargot, scampi or spaghetti sauce.

GREEK SALAD

1 small head iceberg lettuce
1 head romaine lettuce
1/3 head chicory
1 large onion, sliced
1 cup crumbled feta cheese
Dressing

DRESSING

Olive oil
Red wine vinegar
1 to 2 T. oregano

Mix three parts olive oil to one part vinegar. Add 1 to 2 T. oregano and stir.

GARNISH (per salad)

1 tomato wedge
1 sprig watercress
1 radish or carrot curl
2 thin cucumber slices
1 solid square feta cheese
2 anchovy filets

STEAK SOUP

***This is a fine, hearty soup. Served with some bread and salad,
it could be a great main course, especially on a cold winter day.***

2 cloves garlic, minced
1 T. olive oil
3/4 lb. beef tenderloin, cubed
1 1/2 large carrots, diced
1 zucchini, diced
1/2 large onion, cubed
1 T. oregano
Salt and pepper to taste
2 cups water
1 1/2 cups tomato juice
3/4 cup tomato purée
1/2 cup canned tomatoes, diced
1/2 small cabbage, cubed
2 oz. cornstarch diluted in 3/4 cup water
Grated Parmesan cheese

1. In a 4- to 5-quart saucepan sauté the garlic in olive oil. Add the meat
   and sauté until browned.
2. Add carrots, zucchini, onions, oregano, salt and pepper. Braise the
   vegetables.
3. Add the water, tomato juice, tomato purée and diced tomatoes.
   Bring to boil, then reduce heat and simmer 45 minutes or until
   vegetables are tender.
4. Add cabbage; stir ingredients and cook for 3 minutes.
5. Stir in enough of the cornstarch mixture to obtain desired
   consistency. Remove from heat and serve accompanied by the
   grated Parmesan cheese.

FISHMARKET CATFISH

Catfish has not enjoyed a spectacular popularity as a food fish at least in part because of its unorthodox appearance, but it is delicious if prepared properly.

2 lbs. catfish filets
Seasoned flour
2 eggs, beaten
3/4 cup vegetable oil
Dill Sauce
Lemon wedges
Parsley

1. Dust filets with flour. Dip in eggs, then flour again.
2. In a large skillet heat the oil until very hot. Add fish and sauté until golden on both sides, about 7 to 10 minutes. Remove to heated platter.
3. Spoon *Dill Sauce* over fish and garnish with lemon wedges and parsley.

DILL SAUCE

1/4 cup butter
1 T. lemon juice
1/2 t. fresh dill, chopped
1/4 cup *Brown Sauce Demi-Glace*

1. Heat butter and lemon juice.
2. Add dill, stir in *Demi-Glace.* Cook and stir until heated through and blended.

BROWN SAUCE DEMI-GLACE

2 cubes beef bouillon
2 1/2 cups boiling water
2 sprigs parsley
1/4 cup butter
6 T. flour
1 t. soy sauce

1. Dissolve bouillon cubes in boiling water and add parsley. Simmer 10 minutes. Remove parsley and return to boil.
2. In a separate pan, melt butter and stir in flour to make a thick paste. Add this mixture to boiling bouillon; add soy sauce and stir until *Glace* has reached a medium consistency.

NOTE: You may refrigerate extra *Demi-Glace* and serve, after reheating, as a garnish with other seafoods.

ZUCCHINI ALMANDINE

5 medium zucchinis cut into 1/4 inch pieces
1 cup flour
3 eggs, beaten
Peanut oil

1. Flour each zucchini slice and dip into eggs.
2. Quickly sauté in very hot peanut oil.
3. Remove from pan and cover with *Almandine Sauce.*

ALMANDINE SAUCE

1/4 lb. butter
1 cup sliced almonds.

Heat butter in skillet, add almonds and sauté until thoroughly heated.

PAPAYA GERALD

3 papayas
1 quart Haagen Daz French vanilla ice cream

Cut papayas in half and remove seeds. Fill each half with medium scoop of ice cream.

Dinner for Four

Ceviche

Lamb Cazuela

Stuffed Potatoes

Pork with Peanuts

Flan

Beverages:
Pouilly-Fuissé or full bodied beer

Moises Asturrizaga, Owner and Chef

Tucked away in an inconspicuous corner on Chicago's north side is a little restaurant that offers a big adventure in Peruvian dining. Unpretentious yet comfortable, Piqueo has prepared food since 1969 with the kind of finesse and subtlety not always associated with South American cuisine.

Owner Moises Asturrizaga believes that to be successful in the restaurant business one must provide the personal touch. A man of his word, Asturrizaga is not only the congenial host, he also does all of the shopping, is the restaurant's sole chef, and will, upon request, prepare any Peruvian dish to order.

A professional actor and aspiring opera singer in his native Peru, Asturrizaga came to this country with the idea of making just enough money to finance further musical instruction in Milan, Italy. Marriage and a growing fondness for Chicago changed his plans, and in 1969 he opened Piqueo. "Piqueo means 'many dishes, many flavors.' It has been, and will continue to be, my pleasure to live up to that name."

5427 N. Clark Street

CEVICHE

***This is one of Peru's national dishes and an excellent hangover
remedy. It's Peru's answer to Alka Seltzer, only much tastier.***

1 lb. raw turbot or halibut, cleaned, washed and cut into small pieces
1 clove garlic, chopped
1 chili pepper, ground
2 oz. onion, finely chopped
Salt and pepper to taste
Fresh lemons
1 oz. onion, sliced thin
1 chili pepper, sliced
1 T. fresh cilantro, chopped

1. Place fish in a bowl for marinating. Season with the garlic, ground
   chili pepper, chopped onion, salt and pepper. Cover generously
   with lemon juice.
2. Make a dressing of the remaining onion, chili pepper, salt, pepper,
   cilantro and enough lemon juice to cover the fish. Marinate
   2 to 3 hours.
3. Serve with the dressing.

NOTE: It is a good idea to first soak the fish in salted cold water for
       one or two hours in order to remove any oil.

LAMB CAZUELA

1 clove garlic, chopped
1 chili pepper, ground
Salt and pepper to taste
1 t. oregano
1 oz. lard or oil
2 lbs. lamb shoulder, cut in pieces
3 oz. tomatoes, peeled, seeded and chopped
1 T. rice
5 oz. fresh peas
5 oz. string beans
2 oz. celery, chopped
3 oz. turnips, chopped
4 oz. carrots, chopped
1 cob of corn, sliced in circles
1 cabbage leaf, chopped
2 potatoes, peeled and quartered

1. Sauté garlic, chili pepper, salt, pepper and oregano in lard or oil until golden.
2. Add meat to skillet and brown.
3. Add tomatoes, rice, peas, string beans, celery, turnips, carrots, corn and cabbage. Cover skillet and cook over moderate heat, stirring occasionally, for 5 minutes.
4. Add about 4 cups of boiling water and potatoes. Cook over moderate heat until lamb and potatoes are tender, about 20 to 30 minutes.

Two pounds of lamb seems like a lot of meat to use, but this is an old-fashioned, thick, hearty soup and it really is necessary to use that much to achieve the right texture and taste.

STUFFED POTATOES

1 1/2 lbs. potatoes
1 T. flour
1/2 t. salt
1/2 t. pepper
Filling

1. Scrub potatoes and cook, with skins on, in boiling water until tender.

2. Peel the potatoes, then rice or mash them. Stir in flour, salt and pepper.
3. On a lightly floured board, knead the potato mixture about 20 turns or just until easy to handle, like a biscuit dough. Shape into an oblong 14 inches long. Set aside and make *Filling.*

FILLING

3 to 4 T. lard or other fat
3/4 lb. ground beef
2 cloves garlic, crushed
3/4 cup chopped onions
1/2 t. salt
1/4 t. pepper
1/4 t. ground oregano
2 eggs, hardboiled, chopped
1/3 cup seedless raisins
1/4 cup Greek olives, pitted and chopped
1 to 2 t. parsley, chopped
Flour for dredging
Oil for deep frying

1. Melt lard in large skillet and add meat and garlic. Cook over medium heat, stirring frequently, until meat loses its pink color.
2. Add onions, salt, pepper and oregano. Cook, stirring frequently, until onions are transparent, about 7 minutes.
3. Add eggs, raisins, olives and parsley. Cook, stirring, for 1 minute. Remove from heat.
4. Cut potato dough into 2-inch pieces. Make a hollow, or well, in each piece. Fill with a rounded tablespoon of meat mixture. Mold potato mixture around filling and form into ovals.
5. Dredge potatoes in flour. Let dry for 45 minutes.
6. Fry potatoes in deep oil at 360 degrees for 3 to 4 minutes or until golden brown.

NOTE: This may be served with a hot sauce on the side.

PORK WITH PEANUTS

2 lbs. shoulder pork, cut in small chunks
Salt and pepper to taste
Lard or oil
3 cloves garlic, chopped
3 yellow chili peppers, chopped
1 medium onion, cut in thick slices
1 cup toasted peanuts, ground in blender

1. Season the pork with salt and pepper and refrigerate overnight.
2. When ready to prepare, brown pork in hot oil until golden and set aside.
3. In same pan, sauté garlic, chili peppers and onion.
4. Return pork to pan and mix well. Add enough boiling water to cover the mixture and cook over low heat for 15 minutes.
5. Add ground peanuts and continue cooking until tender, 15 to 20 minutes.

FLAN

3 15-oz. cans evaporated milk
2 cups water
1 cup sugar
6 eggs
Sauce

1. Combine all ingredients except *Sauce* and beat until frothy.
2. Pour mixture into a 2-1/2 quart shallow casserole. Place casserole
   in larger pan containing 1 inch of water. Bake at 350 degrees for
   about 50 minutes or until a knife inserted 2 inches from edge
   comes out clean.
3. Remove casserole from water bath. Let cool.
4. Cut into squares and serve with *Sauce*.

SAUCE

1 lb. brown sugar
3 cups water
1 or 2 sticks cinnamon
4 to 6 whole cloves

1. Combine all ingredients in a large, heavy saucepan. Bring to a boil
   and continue boiling for 10 to 15 minutes or until thick.
2. Allow sauce to cool and pour over custard.

***This version is made without the smoky taste some flans have.
I prefer it this way when eating hot, spicy foods.***

Chicago

The Pump Room

Dinner for Six

Oysters Marseilles

Watercress Soup

Pump Room Salad

Veal Piccata

Zucchini Provençal

Peach Calypso

Wines:
With Oysters: Möet et Chandon White Star Extra Dry
With Salad and Entrée: Trefethen Chardonnay, 1975
With Dessert: Wiltinger Scharzberg Auslese, 1976

Lettuce Entertain You Enterprises, Owners

Rich Melman, Chairman

Gambino Sotelino, Executive Chef

To natives and visitors alike, the Pump Room and Chicago are practically synonymous. Since the room opened in 1938 it has been the premier gathering spot for the famous and near famous from the political, entertainment and business worlds.

Originally designed to recreate the atmosphere of the 18th century English night spot of the same name, the Chicago version quickly established its own traditions and an admiring and loyal clientele.

In 1975, the Pump Room was taken over and completely refurbished by a group of local restaurateurs known collectively as Lettuce Entertain You Enterprises. Rich Melman, Chairman of Lettuce Entertain You, says, "I wanted the Pump Room to be very understated, simple, European. Although it seats 230 people, I think the dining room has a cozy feeling. A lot of thought was given to being able to see everyone."

Executive Chef Gambino Sotelino was born in Vigo, Spain where, at twelve, he started to cook in his cousin's restaurant. Subsequently he worked at the Ritz Hotel in Madrid, the Plaza Athéné in Paris, various Hilton Hotels, the Hotel Madison in Washington D.C., and Le Perroquet in Chicago before joining the Pump Room.

1301 N. State Parkway

OYSTERS MARSEILLES

***This is a version of Oysters Rockefeller but the addition of
DeJonghe Butter makes it very special.***

24 large, fresh oysters
Spinach
DeJonghe Butter
Fresh parsley
Lemon wedges

1. Open oysters by inserting an oyster knife near the pointed end of
   the shell. Carefully scrape the oyster meat from one of the shells
   and place it on the other. Discard empty shell. Clean the
   remaining shell of sand and shell pieces.
2. Distribute the cooked spinach evenly among the cleaned oyster shells.
3. Top with 1 T. of the *DeJonghe Butter.*
4. Broil until the butter turns golden brown and the oysters are done,
   about 5 minutes.
5. Garnish with fresh parsley and lemon wedges.

SPINACH

5 oz. fresh spinach
1 T. butter
1 t. Pernod
Salt
White pepper
Nutmeg

1. Trim stems off spinach and wash well to remove any sand. Shake
   off excess water and chop roughly.
2. Melt butter in sauté pan and add spinach.
3. When spinach starts to wilt, add seasonings and Pernod.
4. Cook for 1 additional minute, remove from heat and let cool.

DEJONGHE BUTTER

3/4 lb. unsalted butter
1 1/2 oz. sliced almonds
1 1/2 oz. fresh garlic, peeled
1 1/2 oz. shallots, peeled
3 large sprigs parsley
4 slices white bread, trimmed of crusts and crumbled
2 T. lemon juice
1 T. Pernod
1/2 t. salt
1/4 t. white pepper
1/4 cup whole wheat flour

1. Let butter soften a little at room temperature.
2. Finely chop almonds, garlic, shallots and parsley.
3. Cream butter and add all ingredients until well blended.

WATERCRESS SOUP

Don't be afraid to add more watercress to suit individual taste. Part of being a successful cook is being able to follow your instincts.

3 oz. onion, minced
1 1/2 oz. carrot, minced
2 1/2 oz. butter
7 oz. red potatoes, peeled, sliced thin
Salt and white pepper to taste
1 t. sugar
10 oz. water
5 oz. milk
10 oz. whipping cream
1/2 bunch watercress
2 T. sour cream

1. In a 2-quart pan, sauté onions and carrots in butter until transparent.
2. Add potatoes, salt, sugar and white pepper. Cook for 5 minutes on low heat.
3. Add water, bring to boil, then simmer about 20 minutes or until potatoes are thoroughly cooked.
4. Add milk and cream and bring soup back to boil.
5. Off the heat, strain the vegetables and potatoes out of the soup and place in a blender with a little liquid from the soup. Add the watercress and blend until everything is smoothly puréed. Pour purée back into soup.
6. Mix the soup together with a whisk, beating in the sour cream. Check the seasoning, then cool. Chill the soup well.

This soup has been on the menu since the Pump Room opened and it will probably be there for many years to come.

PUMP ROOM SALAD

2 10 oz. bags spinach, stems trimmed, washed and chopped
3/4 cup radish, finely chopped
3/4 cup green onion tops, chopped
3/4 cup bacon, cooked and crumbled
6 hard boiled eggs, whites and yolks separated and finely chopped

DRESSING

2 T. Grey Poupon mustard
1 t. sugar
Pinch salt
1/4 t. anchovy paste
2/3 cup olive oil
1/4 cup vinegar
2 T. water

1. Put mustard, seasonings and anchovy paste in a bowl and mix well.
2. Whisk in oil gradually, emulsifying.
3. Mix in vinegar and water.

You can really show off with this salad. Line all the ingredients in neat rows in a large salad bowl for presentation. After showing the salad to the diners, pour over enough dressing to coat the ingredients well and toss. Serve on chilled plates.

VEAL PICCATA

Veal is such a versatile meat that a cook can use almost anything as a garnish. We generally use capers, but experiment; try anchovies or fried eggs or a brown sauce added to the pan drippings.

2 1/2 lbs. veal scallops, pounded thin
Flour
Salt and white pepper
3 oz. clarified butter
1 lemon, juiced
1/4 cup capers

1. Season the flour with salt and pepper and lightly flour the veal scallops.
2. Heat clarified butter in a skillet or sauté pan until hot and quickly sauté floured veal scallops on both sides. Remove from pan to serving platter or plates and keep warm.
3. Add lemon juice and capers to butter and drippings in the sauté pan. Heat quickly and pour over veal.

Veal piccata is something of a midwestern favorite. It appears on menus much more frequently here than on the East or West Coasts. It's not a difficult recipe if the cook follows directions.

ZUCCHINI PROVENCAL

Use plenty of garlic in this dish and don't be worried if the zucchini loses some of its color. The zucchini can be slightly overcooked but don't let it get mushy.

1 1/2 lbs. zucchini
1/4 cup onions, minced
2 large cloves garlic, minced
1/4 cup olive oil
Salt, black pepper, sugar to taste
1 bay leaf
1 8-oz. can diced tomatoes
1/2 16-oz. can tomato juice (additional juice optional)
2 anchovy filets
2 oz. white wine
2 t. cornstarch
2 T. water

1. Wash zucchini, remove ends and slice about 1/4 inch thick.
2. Sauté onions and garlic in oil until transparent. Add seasoning and bay leaf.
3. Add canned tomatoes and zucchini, mix gently and simmer until zucchini is cooked, about 15 to 20 minutes, adding more tomato juice if additional liquid is necessary.
4. Whirl anchovies and wine in blender and add to zucchini. Mix cornstarch and water and stir into zucchini until mixture thickens slightly.

PEACH CALYPSO

6 large coconut macaroons
4 T. whipping cream
1 1/2 t. Grand Marnier
1 1/2 t. Kirsch
Pinch salt
6 medium-sized fresh, ripe peaches, cut in half with
   seeds removed
Crème Anglaise

1. Soak macaroons in cream, liqueurs, and a pinch of salt. Mash them
   with a fork.
2. Spoon macaroon mixture into peach cavities and broil 5 minutes
   until golden brown.
3. Put on serving plates and spoon *Creme Anglaise* over them.

CRÈME ANGLAISE

1/2 cup sugar
6 egg yolks
1 cup cream (or half-and-half)
1/2 cup milk
1/4 t. salt
1 1/2 T. Grand Marnier
2 t. Kirsch
1/2 t. vanilla
2 T. sour cream

1. Beat yolks and sugar together.
2. Add cream, milk and salt; cook, stirring over a double boiler
   until thick. Remove from heat.
3. Add liqueurs and vanilla and whisk in sour cream.

THE RITZ-CARLTON

Dinner for Four to Six

*Fricassée de Coquilles St. Jacques
et Polourdes aux Petits Légumes
(Stew of Scallops and Clams
with Garden Vegetables)*

*Crème d'Avocat Froide
(Cold Avocado Cream Soup)*

Veal with Morels

Subric de Haricots Verts

Soufflé Glace Miracle

Wines:
With Scallops: Pouilly-Fumé
With Veal: Château Haut-Gros Caillou
With Soufflé: Korbel Natural

Four Seasons Hotels, Ltd., Operating Owners
Maxime Rochereau, Executive Chef

The elegance and opulence of the Hotel Ritz in Paris forever established the word "ritzy" in English lexicons to mean anything or anyone of similar splendor or deportment. In 1975, The Ritz-Carlton Hotel opened in Chicago's Water Tower Place and both the hotel and The Dining Room were designed to reflect the quality and traditions of its famous Paris cousin.

Probably the most famous tradition of all is the culinary heritage left by Georges Auguste Escoffier, the Ritz's original chef, considered by many to be the greatest chef of all time. "Escoffier single-handedly established the tone and style of the Ritz cuisine. We try to follow his tradition by serving only the finest, most imaginative French food," says Jacquelin Fridrich, director of public relations.

Large beveled mirrors, French pinewood paneling and Louis XIV chairs clearly distinguish The Ritz-Carlton dining room from typical hotel restaurants. The cutlery and chinaware display the famous Ritz crest and traditional Mediterranean blue glassware complete the table settings.

Newly appointed Executive Chef Maxime Rochereau previously headed the kitchen staff at the Breakers Hotel in Palm Beach and has been associated with the Georges Rey and Potiniere du Soir restaurants in New York.

Water Tower Place

FRICASSÉE DE COQUILLES ST. JACQUES ET POLOURDES AUX PETITS LÉGUMES

5 oz. carrots, julienned
5 oz. turnips, julienned
16 fresh clams
1 bottle Muscadet wine, cold
6 oz. butter
3 oz. shallots, chopped
16 oz. heavy cream
16 sea scallops
Peelings of 2 lemons, cut into fine julienne strips
1 small truffle

1. Steam the carrots and turnips for 4 minutes. Set aside.
2. Wash the clams and put them in a pan filled with chilled wine. Simmer for 5 minutes. This will open the clams. Do not boil. Drain and reserve the broth. Remove clams from shells.
3. Melt the butter in a saucepan and add shallots. Sauté quickly, but do not brown them. Add the reserved broth and reduce it almost completely.
4. Add heavy cream and reduce one third.
5. Add scallops and bring mixture to boiling point. Add clams and vegetables and cook for a few minutes more.
6. Serve in onion soup crock. Sprinkle with the lemon peel and decorate with truffle.

Try to use Cape Cod scallops if available. Whatever type you use, be careful not to overcook them. They should be opaque and firm, but not tough.

CRÈME D'AVOCAT FROIDE

2 oz. butter
3 soupspoons flour
1 quart chicken broth
1 pint whipping cream
Salt and white pepper to taste
Juice of 1/2 lemon
2 avocados, peeled and seeded
Unsweetened whipped cream

1. Melt the butter in a saucepan and add flour. Blend with a whisk over low heat for 2 minutes.
2. Add the chicken broth, stir well with whisk and bring to boiling point.
3. In another saucepan, bring the whipping cream to a boil. When boiling, add to chicken broth. Add salt and pepper and the lemon juice. Let mixture boil gently for 10 to 15 minutes, then strain into a container and refrigerate until cold.
4. Process the avocados in a blender to a fine purée. Add to the cold cream of chicken and stir well.
5. Serve in iced cups and top with a dab of the whipped cream.

It is always difficult to make a soup in small quantities, so this recipe will actually make more than you need to serve four or six. I do not suggest freezing the leftovers, but refrigerated, it will make a wonderful addition to tomorrow's lunch.

It is easy to oversalt a cold soup, so be careful. If you're not sure how much to use, wait until it's ready to be served and season slowly.

VEAL WITH MORELS

8 oz. morels
Salt and pepper to taste
Flour for dredging
8 T. butter
12 3-oz. veal scallops
1 t. shallots, chopped
3 oz. red port wine
8 oz. heavy cream
1 t. meat glaze

1. Soak morels in cold water overnight. When ready to use, cut morels in half and wash very well under tap water. Set aside.
2. Salt and pepper the veal and dip in flour. Melt 6 T. butter in sauté pan and cook veal quickly, 1 or 2 minutes on each side. Set aside and keep warm. Reserve pan glaze.
3. Heat 2 T. of butter and add the shallots and morels. Cook for 2 to 3 minutes.
4. Deglaze pan with wine. After a little reduction, add heavy cream and meat glaze. Let boil until a slightly thickened consistency has been obtained.
5. Return the veal to the pan for 1 minute.
6. Serve veal covered with sauce and morels on top.

NOTE: Rice pilaf is an excellent garnish for this dish.

SUBRIC DE HARICOTS VERT

2 lbs. green beans
8 oz. butter, softened
3 eggs, beaten
Salt and pepper to taste

1. Cook the beans for a few minutes in a small amount of water.
   While still hard, grind them, using the small-holed plate of
   your grinder.
2. Mix the beans with butter and eggs, salt and pepper.
3. Grease a baking dish. Pour in bean mixture and cook at
   400 degrees until top achieves a hard consistency.

***Don't overcook the beans! Americans have had a tendency to
turn perfectly delicious vegetables into mush, thus losing the vitamin
content and the taste. Think crisp!***

SOUFFLÉ GLACE MIRACLE

1 pint egg yolks
7 oz. powdered sugar
5 oz. hazelnuts, grated
3 pineapple rings, chopped
3 oz. rum
Juice of 3 lemons
1/2 quart whipped cream
1 oz. cocoa powder

1. Mix egg yolks and 6 oz. powdered sugar. Beat at high speed for 6 minutes.
2. Add hazelnuts, pineapple, rum and lemon juice.
3. Whip the cream just until it stands by itself. Fold it into mixture. Pour into soufflé dish with a 2-inch paper collar. Filling should stand 1 to 1 1/2 inches above rim. Freeze thoroughly.
4. Before serving, remove collar and dust soufflé with mixture of 1 oz. powdered sugar and 1 oz. cocoa powder.

Su Casa

Dinner for Four

Margarita Cocktail

Quesadillas

Steak Ranchero

Refried Beans

Fruit Plate

Café Chiapas

Beverages:
Bohemia Ale or Dos Equis (XX) dark

Ike Sewell, Owner

Carlos Acosta, Chef

The opening of Su Casa in 1962 marked the debut of one of the first authentic Mexican restaurants in Chicago. Housed in the converted stables of a Civil War era townhouse on the city's north side, Su Casa boasts many antique appointments significantly older than the building itself; 16th and 17th century artifacts collected from ancient Mexican haciendas dot the interior. Carved wooden chairs, hand painted tabletop tiles and stained glass windows, all executed by Mexican draftsmen, complete the effect.

When Su Casa opened, ethnic restaurants were only just beginning to enjoy a degree of popularity, and the present chef, Carlos Acosta, admits that Mexican spices were sometimes too hot for American tastes. "We toned down the use of hot peppers because we sometimes got complaints that the food was too spicy. But in the last five to ten years, American tastes have changed and customers occasionally complain that our food isn't spicy enough. For those who like their dishes ultra-hot, we provide extra condiments on the table."

Chef Acosta was born in Guadalajara, Mexico and came to this country in 1968. Before joining the staff of Su Casa in 1973, he worked as chef at Northwestern University, various country clubs and for the Marriott Hotel chain.

49 E. Ontario Street

MARGARITA COCKTAIL

Lemon or lime peel
Bar salt
1 1/2 oz. tequila
3/4 oz. Cointreau
1/2 oz. lemon or lime juice
Crushed ice

1. Rub the rim of a chilled glass with the peel from the lemon or lime and dip into bar salt.
2. Place tequila, Cointreau and juice into shaker filled with crushed ice. Shake well.
3. Strain the mixture in the shaker into glass.

Most bartenders use tequila and triple sec in a margarita but we think that makes it too thick and sweet. We prefer to use Cointreau.

QUESADILLAS

8 corn tortillas
16 oz. Chihuahua cheese, grated
Sauce

1. Heat a skillet and place tortilla in center.
2. Place 2 oz. of the grated cheese on tortilla. When the cheese has melted, fold tortilla over in half.
3. Cook about 3 minutes on each side. Remove from heat and serve with *Sauce* on the side.

SAUCE

Oil
14 oz. fresh or canned tomatillo
1 clove garlic, chopped
4 oz. onions, chopped
2 t. cilantro, chopped
1 jalapeño pepper, chopped
Salt to taste

1. In a little oil, sauté tomatillos until clear. Dispose of liquid.

2. Add garlic, onions, cilantro, jalapeño and salt. Mix well and remove from heat. Allow to cool before serving.

NOTE: Chihuahua cheese is usually available in most Mexican specialty stores. If unavailable, Muenster may be substituted.

STEAK RANCHERO

Oil
1 1/2 lb. flank steak, cut crosswise
2 green peppers, sliced
1 large onion, cut julienne style
2 tomatoes, diced
1 jalapeño pepper, chopped
1 clove garlic, chopped
4 oz. cilantro, chopped
Salt to taste
1 cup beef stock or water

1. Heat oil in a skillet and add flank steak. Brown well.
2. Add vegetables and seasonings and cook briefly.
3. Add beef stock or water and simmer for 15 minutes.

REFRIED BEANS

The name means exactly what it says: refried. Mexicans often cook enough for two or three days. For each meal, the beans are refried and the process may be repeated four or five times. They actually do get better so don't be afraid to try it.

1 cup pinto beans
1/2 cup lard

1. Boil the beans until soft, about 35 to 40 minutes.
2. Mash the beans thoroughly.
3. Put lard in skillet and heat. When very hot, pour in mashed beans and fry, stirring frequently, for 20 to 25 minutes.

If you have any remaining Chihuahua cheese you may add it to the beans as a garnish.

FRUIT PLATE

1 mango, skinned and sliced
1 papaya, skinned, sliced and seeded
1/4 watermelon, sliced
Dessert Sauce

Arrange fruit on a plate and cover with *Dessert Sauce.*

SAUCE

1/2 cup whipped cream
3 T. honey
3 T. maraschino cherry juice
2 T. mayonnaise
1/2 lemon

1. Blend the whipped cream and honey into a smooth mixture.
2. Add cherry juice and mayonnaise and mix well.
3. Squeeze juice from lemon and blend into cream mixture.

Try to use tropical fruits if they are available, but you can substitute with peaches, cantaloupe, grapes or any of your favorite fruits.

CAFÉ CHIAPAS

Coffee
1/2 oz. Kahlua
1/2 oz. brandy
1 cinnamon stick
Whipped cream

Add Kahlua and brandy to coffee, drop in cinnamon stick and top off with a dab of whipped cream.

This is Mexico's answer to Irish coffee.

Dinner for Six

Fresh North Atlantic Sea Scallops Tango

Fresh Basil and Tomato Soup

Caesar Salad

Fresh Sea Bass En Croûte
With Mousse of Fresh Salmon and Shrimp
Port Wine Mushroom Sauce

Potato Skins

Fresh Raspberries
With Raspberry Liqueur

Wines:

With Scallops and Soup: Gewürztraminer
Trimbach, 1975

With Entrée: Meursault Ropiteau, 1976

With Dessert: Edelwein Gold, Freemark Abbey, 1976

George Badonsky, Owner

John Stoltzman, Executive Chef

"As strange as it seems now, Tango was a very controversial place when it opened," says owner George Badonsky. "We dared to offer great seafood prepared in the French manner, served in an unpretentious way and set in a contemporary environment."

The controversy has long since died down and Tango has firmly established itself as one of Chicago's best restaurants. "While I am gratified by Tango's popularity, I know that a restaurant should never get too comfortable with success," says Badonsky. "Innovation and change are essential."

Tango's selections do, in fact, change frequently and often include seafood previously unknown or ignored by midwestern palates. "With shipments of fresh fish flying in two or three times a week, there's no reason why Chicagoans can't enjoy the variety previously reserved for communities located on the eastern or western seaboards."

Tango is justifiably noted for its seafood, but it also offers a large complement of alternate choices. Executive Chef John Stoltzman, who has been at Tango since 1973, comes well prepared to handle the challenge. A graduate of the Washburn Trade School's chef training program, Stoltzman apprenticed at Maxim's and served as chef at the Flying Frenchman before assuming his duties at Tango.

3172 N. Sheridan Road

FRESH NORTH ATLANTIC SEA
SCALLOPS TANGO

2 lbs. fresh sea scallops
1/2 cup lemon juice
1/2 cup lime juice
1/3 cup olive oil
1 t. minced garlic
2 t. salt
White pepper to taste
1 red onion, chopped
2 green peppers, diced
1 pint cherry tomatoes, halved
1/2 cup black olives, halved
Lettuce leaves
Parsley

1. Cut scallops in half and place in shallow glass bowl.
2. Add lemon juice, lime juice, olive oil, garlic, salt and pepper.
   Marinate overnight, making sure scallops are completely covered
   by marinade.
3. Add chopped onion, green pepper, cherry tomatoes and black olives.
   Mix well and chill.
4. When ready to serve, place mixture on lettuce leaves and sprinkle
   with chopped, fresh parsley.

NOTE: You may substitute bay scallops for the sea scallops; they are
       slightly smaller but otherwise just as good.

FRESH BASIL AND TOMATO SOUP

3 T. olive oil
1 T. minced garlic
10 ripe tomatoes, peeled and diced
2 quarts chicken stock
25 fresh basil leaves
Salt
White pepper
Garlic croutons
Parsley

1. Heat oil in a saucepan and sauté garlic. Add tomatoes and cook on low heat for 30 minutes.
2. Add chicken stock, basil, salt and pepper and simmer for 30 minutes. Taste for seasoning.
3. Serve with croutons and fresh parsley.

Since fresh basil is usually available these days, don't use dried basil unless you absolutely have to. You'll lose too much flavor for the sake of convenience.

FRESH SEA BASS EN CROÛTE WITH
MOUSSE OF FRESH SALMON AND SHRIMP
PORT WINE MUSHROOM SAUCE

This whole recipe can be made the day before which makes it perfect for company. Keep everything refrigerated until you are ready for your final preparations, then simply reheat the *Mushroom Sauce* and bake the *Bass En Croûte* as you would normally.

2 lbs. fresh sea bass filets
1 cup dry white wine
1 cup water
6 shallots, sliced
Salt and white pepper
Puff pastry, homemade or store bought
Salmon Mousse with Shrimp
2 egg yolks

1. Poach the bass in a mixture of wine, water, shallots, salt and pepper. Remove the bass, allow it to cool and flake it apart with a fork.
2. Meanwhile, roll out puff pastry to a 1/8 inch thickness and cut out 12 4x4 inch squares.
3. Place about 4 oz. of the *Salmon and Shrimp Mousse* in the center of 6 of the squares. Divide the bass into 6 portions and place them on top of the *Salmon and Shrimp Mousse.*
4. Brush the bottom edge of the pastry with egg yolk. Place top pastry on and pinch the two together. Refrigerate until ready to use.
5. Bake at 375 degrees for 10 to 15 minutes or until light brown. Serve with *Port Wine Mushroom Sauce.*

SALMON MOUSSE WITH SHRIMP

1 lb. fresh salmon, boned
1 t. salt
1/4 t. white pepper
3 egg whites
1 cup heavy cream
1 lb. shrimp, cooked, cleaned and diced

1. Grind salmon through a fine-holed grinder.
2. Place ground fish, salt and pepper in a food processor or blender for 30 to 45 seconds. Add egg whites and blend for 1 minute.
3. With processor running slowly, add heavy cream. Blend for 30 seconds.
4. Remove mixture from blender and blend in shrimp. Refrigerate until needed.

PORT WINE MUSHROOM SAUCE

2 T. chopped shallots
8 T. butter
2 cups fresh mushrooms, sliced
3 cups port wine
2 cups *Fish Velouté*
Salt and pepper

1. Sauté shallots in 4 T. butter. Add mushrooms and port wine. Reduce sauce by one-half.
2. Add *Fish Velouté* and simmer for 20 minutes.
3. Taste for seasoning, adding salt and pepper if necessary. If sauce is too thick, add more wine.
4. Finish sauce by adding remaining butter.

FISH VELOUTÉ

2 T. butter
2 T. flour
2 cups fish stock (cold)
Salt and pepper to taste

1. Melt butter in saucepan and add flour to make a roux. Cook until light golden.
2. Add cold fish stock and blend with a whisk until smooth. Add salt and pepper and cook for approximately 20 minutes, stirring occasionally.
3. Strain through a fine sieve.

CAESAR SALAD

1 t. anchovy paste
1 t. minced garlic
1/2 t. salt
4 T. black pepper
1 1/2 t. Dijon mustard
1/2 t. Worcestershire sauce
2 whole, raw eggs
8 T. olive oil
4 T. malt vinegar
1 lemon, juiced
2 heads romaine lettuce, washed and dried
1 cup croutons
1/2 cup Parmesan cheese

1. Mix anchovy paste, garlic, salt, pepper, mustard, Worcestershire sauce and eggs in a bowl.
2. Add oil, vinegar and lemon juice and taste mixture for seasoning.
3. Just before serving, toss lettuce with dressing. Add croutons and toss again. Serve on chilled plates.

POTATO SKINS

6 large baking potatoes
Oil for deep frying
Sour cream
Applesauce

1. Bake the potatoes thoroughly.
2. When cool, cut the potatoes in half, then in quarters. Clean almost all of the potato out of the skin and save for other uses.
3. When ready to serve, deep fry the skins at 375 degrees until brown and crisp.
4. Serve with sour cream and applesauce.

FRESH RASPBERRIES IN RASPBERRY LIQUEUR

A tip of the toque blanche to Mies van der Rohe who once said 'less is more.' This dessert is the epitome of simplicity, but the perfect ending to a delicious meal.

Cover individual portions of fresh raspberries with the raspberry liqueur of your choice.

Dinner for Four

Quenelle of Pike

Consommé au Truffles

Quatre Cailles en Poèlon
(Quails with Truffles Stuffing)

Truffles' Mixed Vegetables

Arlequin Soufflé

Wines:

With Pike: Puligny-Montrachet, Maison Armand Roux

With Entrèe: Château Bellegrave, Pauillac
Cru Classé Superieur

Chateau Margaux, Premier Grand Cru Classe, 1971

Hyatt Regency, Chicago, Owner
Hans Durst, Executive Chef

"Prepare a few things perfectly" is the official Truffles motto and philosophy. Accordingly, only twelve entrèes appear on its dinner menu and the perfection of their preparation is attested to by the four stars awarded Truffles by the Mobil Travel Guide, one of only three Chicago restaurants so honored.

The restaurant is named, of course, after the rare Perigourdine fungus, which is highlighted as a spectacular appetizer served marinated in champagne and cognac, baked in a crust and served with a truffles sauce.

Located in the Hyatt Regency Hotel just off Michigan Avenue, Truffles has, since its debut in 1974, proved itself comparable to any French restaurant in the country. "The restaurant standard in Chicago is very, very high," says food and beverage director Heinz Kern. "Connoisseurs of fine food no longer have to travel to New York or Paris to sample the best in haute cuisine. It's right here at Truffles."

Executive chef Hans Durst was born near Cologne, Germany and began his cooking apprenticeship at thirteen. Since coming to the United States, he has served as executive chef at the Astroworld Hotel in Houston, the Warwick Hotel, also in Houston, the Fairmont Hotel in Tulsa, and as Chef Tournant at the Hilton Hotel in Washington, D.C.

Hyatt Regency Hotel, 151 East Wacker Drive

QUENELLE OF PIKE

1/2 lb. boneless, raw pike
2 oz. fat salt pork
1/8 t. salt
1/16 t. ground white pepper
1/16 t. ground nutmeg
1 cup fresh bread crumbs
1 egg white
2 oz. whipping cream
Poaching Liquid

1. Place fish and salt pork through a meat grinder twice, using the finest blade.
2. Add bread crumbs and seasonings and beat well.
3. Whip egg white and fold into mixture. Add heavy cream.
4. Test the consistency of the mixture by poaching in simmering water. If it disintegrates, add more egg whites. If the mixture is too dry, whip in a small amount of cream.
5. Mold quenelles in a tablespoon and poach in *Poaching Liquid* until done, about 10 minutes.

POACHING LIQUID

2 quarts fish stock
1 parsley stem
1 bay leaf
1 carrot, chopped
1 stalk celery, chopped
1 onion, chopped
Whole peppercorns

There is no flour in this recipe which simplifies everything because flour is the biggest single problem in any recipe. There's too much chemistry involved. Too little or too much and you've spoiled everything.

CONSOMMÉ AU TRUFFLES

1 lb. lean ground beef
1 leek, chopped
1 carrot, chopped
1/2 onion, diced medium
6 parsley stems
1/2 oz. dried Chinese mushroom
2 egg whites
1 T. whole peppercorns
2 quarts beef stock (cold)
1 whole truffle

1. Mix beef, vegetables, egg whites and peppercorns.
2. Skim off all fat from the stock and add to other ingredients.
   Simmer slowly for 1 hour.
3. Cool, remove meat and vegetables and strain through 2 thicknesses
   of fine cheesecloth.
4. Serve with thin slices of whole truffle.

NOTE: Add a little Cognac or dry sherry if desired.

QUATRE CAILLES EN POELON

4 quail
Stuffing
Quail Sauce

QUAIL

Salt and pepper to taste
Slices of salt pork or back fat
Cheesecloth

1. De-bone the quail completely except for the lower bone in the drumstick. Reserve bones.
2. Sprinkle quail lightly with salt and pepper and fill cavities with *Stuffing.*
3. Cover breasts with fat slices and wrap cheesecloth around each one. Place in buttered roasting pan. Roast uncovered in preheated 450 degree oven for 20 minutes.
4. Cover each quail with *Sauce.*

STUFFING

2 cups day-old bread crumbs
Milk
1 t. shallots, finely chopped
3 oz. butter
6 oz. chicken livers, diced
Salt and pepper to taste
2 egg yolks
Angostura bitters to taste
1 medium truffle with juice, finely diced

1. In a bowl, soak the bread crumbs in enough milk to cover them.
2. In a skillet, sauté the shallots in the butter until they are tender. Stir in chicken livers and cook mixture, stirring, until the livers are slightly browned.
3. Squeeze milk from the bread crumbs and add crumbs to the liver mixture, stirring until it thickens. Season with salt and pepper and remove from heat. Chill for 2 hours.
4. Stir in egg yolks and angostura bitters. Mix in truffle and stuff into quail.

SAUCE

Quail bones
1/2 large onion, chopped
1/2 large carrot, chopped
1 stalk celery, chopped
5 whole peppercorns
3 t. butter
2 oz. Burgundy
1 t. flour
1 pinch thyme
1 pinch marjoram
1 1/2 cups quail or chicken stock
Salt and pepper to taste
1/2 oz. Cognac

1. Sauté bones, onions, carrots, celery and peppercorns in butter until brown.
2. Add wine and reduce completely. Add flour, thyme and marjoram. Continue cooking until flour is light brown, stirring constantly.
3. Add quail or chicken stock. Simmer for 30 minutes, skimming as needed. Remove from heat and strain. Return to heat and bring to boil. Adjust seasoning with salt and pepper. Simmer for 5 minutes and add Cognac.

I can't overemphasize the need for common sense in successful food preparation. Professionals know by instinct or experience when to add something to a recipe and when to omit it. Too many cooks at home stick too closely to the exact recipe and that's where failures occur.

TRUFFLES' MIXED VEGETABLES

1/2 head Chinese cabbage, chopped
1/4 cup carrots, julienned
1 cup Chinese pea pods
1 T. butter
1/2 cup mushrooms, sliced
1 1/2 cups bean sprouts
1/2 pint cherry tomatoes
2 oz. miniature corn-on-the-cob (canned,
    but *not* the pickled cocktail variety)
Salt and pepper to taste
Dressing

DRESSING

1/2 cup oyster sauce
1/2 cup sugar
1/4 t. MSG
1 1/2 cups soy sauce
Salt and pepper to taste

Blend all ingredients thoroughly and set aside until needed.

Cooking procedures—

1. Sauté Chinese cabbage, carrots and pea pods in butter until three-fourths cooked. Add mushrooms, bean sprouts, tomatoes and corn. Season lightly.
2. Pour enough dressing mixture over vegetables to coat well. Simmer for 2 minutes, taking care not to overcook the vegetables. They should remain crisp and crunchy. Serve immediately.

ARLEQUIN SOUFFLÉ

1 T. pineapple, chopped
1 strawberry, chopped
1 oz. Grand Marnier
3/4 cup milk
1 1/2 t. vanilla extract
3 T. butter, melted
6 T. flour
4 large eggs, separated
6 T. sugar
Pinch of salt

1. Put pineapple and strawberry in a bowl. Add Grand Marnier and marinate for 20 minutes.
2. Heat milk in a saucepan. Add vanilla extract.
3. Combine butter and flour and mix until flour is well blended, forming a thick roux. Add heated milk all at once and return mixture to saucepan. Cook over low heat, stirring and beating, until mixture pulls away from sides of the pan. (Use a wire whisk during the first part of the cooking period and then use a wooden spoon, beating vigorously.)
4. Transfer the dough to a 2-quart mixing bowl. While it is still hot, beat in 4 egg yolks, one at a time, being sure that each yolk is thoroughly incorporated before adding another. Add 5 T. of the sugar, one at a time.
5. Add salt to the 4 egg whites and beat them until they stand in soft, stiff peaks. Beat in remaining tablespoon of sugar and continue beating until egg whites stand in sharp, stiff peaks.
6. Stir 2 T. of the beaten egg whites into the dough mixture. Add the pineapple and strawberry, then fold in remaining egg whites, avoiding a beating or stirring motion.
7. Butter a 1 1/2 quart soufflé dish or mold with a center tube. Sprinkle the bottom and sides lightly with sugar. Pour in soufflé mixture. Place mold in a pan with 1 1/2 inches of hot water. Bake soufflé in a preheated 350 degree oven for 50 to 60 minutes or until a cake tester or toothpick inserted in the center comes out clean.
8. Let soufflé stand a few minutes, then unmold onto a round serving plate. Serve immediately.

It is very helpful to know how a recipe is supposed to come out. Cooking "blind" makes everything more difficult. Knowing how a dish is supposed to look, taste and be served is an invaluable asset to your own success.

ENTREES

SALADS

SAUCES AND SPECIAL SEASONINGS

SOUPS

VEGETABLES AND SIDE DISHES

A Collection of Gourmet Recipes
From the Finest Chefs in the Country!

If you enjoyed **Dining In—Chicago** , additional volumes are now available:

Please send me the quantity checked:

_____Dining In—San Francisco
_____Dining In—Chicago
_____Dining In—Houston

_____Dining In—Seattle
_____Dining In—Minneapolis/St. Paul

(and available by June 1979)

_____Dining In—Los Angeles
_____Dining In—San Diego

_____Dining In—Dallas
_____Dining In—Monterey Peninsula

TO ORDER SEND $7.95 PLUS $1.00 POSTAGE AND HANDLING FOR EACH BOOK

ORDER FORM

B I L L   T O

name _____

address _____

city _____ state_____ zip_____

| PAYMENT | CHARGE | |
_____ENCLOSED _____TO:

Visa # _____ Exp.date _____
Master Chg.# _____ Exp.date _____
Signature_____

S H I P   T O

name _____
address_____
city _____
state & zip _____ _____

name _____
address_____
city _____
state & zip _____ _____

Peanut Butter Publishing, Peanut Butter Towers
2733 - 4th Ave. So., Seattle, WA 98134